A STRATEGY FOR HIGHER EDUCATION INTO THE 1990s

THE UNIVERSITY GRANTS COMMITTEE'S ADVICE

September 1984

Ministry of Education, Ontario
Information Centre, 13th Floor,
Mowat Block, Queen's Park,
Toronto, Ont.   M7A 1L2

LONDON: HER MAJESTY'S STATIONERY OFFICE

© Crown Copyright 1984
First published 1984
Third impression 1984
ISBN 0 11 270551 0

UNIVERSITY GRANTS COMMITTEE
14 Park Crescent, London W1N 4DH
Telephone 01-636 7799

From the Chairman
Sir Peter Swinnerton-Dyer FRS

The Rt Hon Sir Keith Joseph Bt MP
Secretary of State for Education and Science
Elizabeth House
York Road
London SE1 7PH

16 August 1984

Dear Secretary of State

DEVELOPMENT OF A STRATEGY FOR HIGHER EDUCATION INTO THE 1990s

In your letters of 14 July 1982 and 1 September 1983 you asked the University Grants Committee for advice on the development of a strategy for higher education into the 1990s and raised a number of questions about the funding, the size and the academic organisation of the university system in Great Britain. I now submit the Committee's response. We hope that we shall have an opportunity to discuss it with you before you take decisions on a strategy for higher education.

By tradition the Committee consults the universities before advising the Government on the future development of the system. Our consultations on this occasion have been more open and extensive than ever before. We initiated the process with our Circular Letter 16/83, dated 1 November 1983 (Annex A). This was formally addressed to the Vice-Chancellors and Principals of the institutions on our grant list. At the request of the Northern Ireland Office we also sent it to the universities in Northern Ireland. For the first time we invited replies not only from the statutory bodies of universities but also from groups and individuals within universities. In addition we encouraged many bodies in the United Kingdom with an interest in higher education to respond. It was open to anybody else who wished to submit views to do so.

We received 658 replies: 55 from the institutions on our grant list and the Northern Ireland universities; 370 from groups within those institutions; 115 from national organisations in higher education, inter-university bodies, professional institutions, trade unions etc; and 118 from individuals, mainly from within universities. Our own sub-committees also gave us their advice, some of them after consulting appropriate professional and other bodies.

Those who responded to the Circular Letter are listed in Annex B and a summary of their views appears as Annex C. We are extremely grateful to them for the care and time they devoted to replying to our questions. Their replies have greatly helped us in reaching our own conclusions and they give a valuable picture of informed opinion about higher education today and about its future needs. The great majority of our respondents have said that they are content for their letters to be accessible to any who wish to study them. We hope you will agree that copies of these letters should be deposited in the libraries of the House of Commons and of the Department of Education and Science.

Our consultations included meetings with representatives of the Committee of Vice-Chancellors and Principals, the National Union of Students, the Association of University Teachers, the Trade Union Side of the Central Council for Non-Teaching Staffs in Universities, the Research Councils and the Boards of the National Advisory Body for Local Authority Higher Education (NAB) and the Wales Advisory Body (WAB). The meetings with NAB require special mention because NAB has been engaged on a parallel exercise in respect of the public sector in England. We have agreed with NAB on a joint statement on the aims and objectives of higher education and we intend to hold further meetings to discuss matters of common concern.

Although we received many useful contributions from those concerned with higher education in Scotland, there was no body corresponding to NAB and WAB with which to consult directly. While we were in the final stages of preparing our advice the Secretary of State for Scotland established a Scottish Tertiary Education Advisory Council. Its first task is "to consider and report on the future strategy for higher education in Scotland, including the arrangements for providing institutions with financial support, and the general principles which should govern relationships between universities and other institutions". We look forward to discussing these matters with the Council.

We regard the submission of this advice as one stage in a continuing process of discussion on the future development of higher education. We hope you will agree that it should be published as soon as possible.

Yours sincerely

Peter Swinnerton-Dyer

ENCS:

A STRATEGY FOR HIGHER EDUCATION INTO THE 1990s:
The University Grants Committee's advice

Contents

Page

Higher education and the needs of society: a joint statement by the University Grants Committee and the National Advisory Body for Local Authority Higher Education — 1

Section 1	Introduction	4
2	Student numbers	7
3	Subject balance and the shift to science and technology	10
4	Teaching	12
5	Research	15
6	Academic standards	20
7	Staffing	22
8	Finance	27
9	Alternative sources of funding	34
10	The organisation of individual universities	39
11	The organisation of higher education: national level	41
12	Summary of recommendations	45
Annex A	UGC Circular Letter 16/83, 1 November 1983	47
B	Respondents to UGC Circular Letter 16/83	51
C	Digest of replies to UGC Circular Letter 16/83	58
D	Comments on statistical projections of student numbers	69
E	Projections of university academic staff numbers	71
F	UGC equipment grant to universities	74
G	Background statistical tables	75

Higher Education and the needs of society

(A joint statement by the University Grants Committee and the National Advisory Body for Local Authority Higher Education, in which 'we' refers to both bodies)

1   More than twenty years ago the Robbins Committee identified four objectives essential to the higher education system. These it described as instruction in skills; promotion of the general powers of the mind; the advancement of learning; and the transmission of a common culture and common standards of citizenship. The meaning given to some of these terms and the context in which they might apply have changed since the time of the Robbins report. Nevertheless, we believe they form an appropriate basis for considering the present and future role of higher education in our society.

2   Providing instruction in skills and promoting the powers of the mind remain the main teaching purposes of higher education. In carrying out this role, higher education attempts to meet both the needs of the economy for highly skilled manpower and the aspirations of individuals for an educational experience which will provide for personal development and lead to a fulfilling and rewarding career. The faster pace of scientific, technological and economic change which our society now experiences has implications for the types of skill which higher education attempts to inculcate.

3   Specific knowledge quickly becomes outdated and the context in which it is applied rapidly changes. Initial higher education, particularly at diploma and first degree level, should therefore emphasise underlying intellectual, scientific and technological principles rather than provide too narrow a specialist knowledge. The abilities most valued in industrial, commercial and professional life as well as in public and social administration are the transferable intellectual and personal skills. These include the ability to analyse complex issues, to identify the core of a problem and the means of solving it, to synthesise and integrate disparate elements, to clarify values, to make effective use of numerical and other information, to work cooperatively and constructively with others, and, above all perhaps, to communicate clearly both orally and in writing. A higher education system which provides its students with these skills is serving society well.

4   The world has changed since Robbins reported. The focus of initial higher education must now be broader and the recent increased emphasis on continuing education must be maintained and accelerated. Many commentators have written about a new industrial revolution, based on information technology, biotechnology and other scientific advances. The need for updating, refreshment and reorientation and for the development of new skills and attitudes is more pervasive and in a sense more mundane. It affects, for example, the professions seeking to cope not only with technological advance, but also with changes in their legislative and regulatory framework; management and trades unions seeking to understand and adapt to their changing social and economic environment; those in the public services absorbing new ideas on the orientation and organisation of their work; and the unemployed seeking to re-enter the labour market in new fields of employment.

5   Continuing education needs to be fostered not only for its essential role in promoting economic prosperity but also for its contribution to personal development and social progress. It can renew personal confidence, regenerate the human spirit and restore a sense of purpose to people's lives through the cultivation of new interests. In short, both effective economic performance and harmonious social relationships depend on our ability to deal successfully with the changes and uncertainties which are now ever-present in our personal and working lives. That is the primary role which we see for continuing education.

6   We have considered whether this increased emphasis on continuing education should be seen as a reinterpretation of Robbins's first two objectives or as a new objective. In view of the importance we attach to continuing education, we see merit in emphasising the establishment of a new objective rather than simply reinterpreting those enumerated over twenty years ago. This we would define as:

The provision of continuing education in order to facilitate adjustment to technological, economic and social change and to meet individual needs for personal development.

7   In concentrating on the teaching functions of higher education the Robbins Committee's first two objectives answer in part the question "What is higher education for?" They do not answer the question "Who is higher education for?" The approach of the Robbins Committee to this question was enshrined in the famous axiom that courses of higher education should be available for all those who are qualified by ability and attainment to pursue them and who wish to do so. This has been the guiding principle of higher education planning for the past two decades.

8   We reaffirm the importance of access and the provision of opportunity. However, the Robbins axiom should be interpreted as broadly as possible, particularly in relation to the term "qualified". Essentially a student's qualification is used to form a judgement on his or her ability to benefit from a course. Yet evidence shows that school examinations such as A-levels are not always good predictors of achievement in higher education and that other qualities and experience can be important determinants of success. We believe that the Robbins axiom is more appropriately restated as:

Courses of higher education should be available for all those who are able to benefit from them and who wish to do so.

9   The third objective of the Robbins Committee refers to the advancement of learning. The extension and application of knowledge are at the heart of the educational process: indeed, that process is itself most vital when it partakes of the nature of discovery. Moreover, through its research activity, higher education makes a major contribution to the continued health of the nation's industry and commerce. To curtail research would in the long run impoverish the nation materially as well as culturally.

10   The language of Robbins's final objective — the transmission of a common culture and common standards of citizenship — may seem somewhat dated nowadays when so much emphasis is placed on the contribution which diverse cultures can make to the vitality and strength of our society. Yet it is still true that there are common values which education seeks to transmit and which help to give society its cohesion and stability. These include the need to protect the free expression and the testing of ideas, and the examination of cases and arguments on their merits. In this sense the objective is even more relevant in today's multi-cultural society than it was twenty years ago. The Robbins Committee's own elaboration of the objective indicates that the sentiments which underlie it still apply today: "This function, important at all times, is perhaps especially important in an age that has set for itself the ideal of equality of opportunity. It is not merely by providing places for students from all classes that this ideal will be achieved, but also by providing, in the atmosphere of the institutions in which the students live and work, influences that in some measure compensate for any inequalities of home background. These influences are not limited to the student population. Universities and colleges have an important role to play in the general cultural life of the communities in which they are situated".

11   The principle of access which we reaffirmed and reformulated above is concerned with providing places for students from different backgrounds and attempting to compensate for previous inequalities. We would broaden it and include students not only from different social classes, but also from different ethnic groups. Moreover, opportunities for women must be as good as opportunities for men. The principle is also concerned with the relationship between each institution and its locality. It is as important as ever that institutions should contribute to the cultural life of their communities. In the world of the 1980s, it is equally important to contribute to the economic, industrial and commercial life of the locality.

12   A longer-term strategy must build on the strengths of the two sectors of higher education and must maintain the present diversity of provision. Full-time first degree courses will continue to be a major activity of both universities and major public sector institutions. Although most subjects of study are available in both sectors, we do not consider that there is any general problem of duplication in view of the spread of institutions and of differences in the structure of courses and in the students

attracted to them. Areas of excessive or inadequate provision will need to be considered by both sides of higher education together; so far as England is concerned, we intend to do it jointly. We would expect the universities to continue to be responsible for the bulk of postgraduate provision, particularly full-time courses and postgraduate work designed to prepare students for careers in research. The public sector should continue to provide the bulk of non-degree courses and of part-time courses. But where there is clear evidence of demand, institutions in either sector should not be prevented from introducing courses which arise from and are connected to their existing offerings.

13   For the public sector, continuing education has always been as important as the education of school-leavers. Universities have varied very much in their involvement. The expansion of continuing education which we believe to be necessary will offer a challenge to both sectors and should be based on their different experiences and strengths. It must take account of the contribution of the Open University.

14   The general leadership of the universities in research work is recognised and reflected in the funding arrangements for the two sectors, but we agree that there is a legitimate research role for major public sector institutions, both to support and sustain teaching and as a contribution to the advancement and application of knowledge.

Section 1

Introduction

1.1 The United Kingdom has a university system of outstanding quality. The universities provide the bulk of the country's science and engineering graduates and research workers, as well as qualified graduates for medicine, law, architecture and numerous other professions. They protect, develop and transmit much of our cultural heritage and carry out most of the country's fundamental research. It is from the universities that the leaders of our industries, professions and national life are predominantly recruited. The rest of the educational system largely depends on the universities for the quality of its teaching staff. Any policy that diminished the role and status of the universities would damage many aspects of our educational, cultural and industrial life.

1.2 Courses in our universities are shorter than in other countries but because of the emphasis placed here on teaching in small groups, the standards are among the highest in the world. The cost *per graduate* is low, even though it includes substantial provision for research. (International comparisons of cost *per student* are misleading, because of the number of students included in the statistics for many other countries who are not seriously or actively pursuing their studies.) The international standing of our university system is demonstrated by the number of overseas countries which have emulated it and by the numbers of overseas students who come to the United Kingdom. Many of these students later reach positions of political and commercial leadership and many of our own graduates teach overseas. All this strengthens the influence of the United Kingdom world-wide and powerfully assists its overseas operations in an increasingly difficult and complex world trading market.

1.3 In our joint statement with the National Advisory Body for Local Authority Higher Education we discuss the four objectives of higher education which the Robbins Committee identified. We believe that these are still valid and that a fifth objective which emphasises the importance of continuing education should be added to them. The principle that "courses of higher education should be available to all those who are able to benefit from them and who wish to do so" should be interpreted as widely as possible. Robbins believed that increasing the numbers of students whose capacity and intellect had been sharpened and developed by higher education would lead to sustained economic development which in turn would justify the expenditure. Since then it has become clear that widespread higher education is a necessary but not a sufficient condition for economic growth. Industry and commerce have acquired more technological and managerial sophistication over the past twenty years — and will need to acquire yet more in the next ten years if they are to survive. The graduates they now need must be able to cope with, and use effectively, the new technologies which pervade all branches of economic activity. Such graduates need as much ability as their predecessors, but far more relevant knowledge.

1.4 At present there are sufficient graduates for many areas of employment; but even in the present depressed economy there is an evident shortage of, for example, electronic engineers and computer scientists. The areas of shortage will change with the years but the imperfections of manpower planning mean that there will always be shortages in key areas unless there is a surplus of graduates overall. Over the next decade, the Government is assuming that Gross Domestic Product will grow between 20 and 25 per cent (*The Next Ten Years: Public Expenditure and Taxation into the 1990s* Cmnd 9189, March 1984). This cannot be achieved without more skilled manpower. Moreover, there will be shifts in employment opportunities. The production of North Sea oil and gas will begin to decline before the end of the 1980s and will need to be replaced by other means of wealth creation. The manufacture of goods will need fewer (but relatively more skilled) employees, while more skilled people will be needed to provide improved services in, for example, education, medicine and recreational activities.

1.5 In Section 2 we discuss recent projections of the demand for higher education. We recommend that the number of full-time and sandwich students in higher education should rise from 560,000 in 1983-84 to about 600,000 in 1989-90. We make no recommendation on how this total should be divided between the universities and the public sector, but clearly numbers in each sector should increase. The number of full-time postgraduate students in universities should rise from 31,000 to 36,000. Because of uncertainties in the present projections of demand, new ones should be made in three to four years' time as a basis for planning in the 1990s. We expect that the national need for graduates will then be growing and that, although the number of school-leavers will be falling, the proportion wishing to enter higher education will be increasing.

1.6   In the universities we expect there to be some shift towards the sciences, and even more towards engineering, in accord with national need; but additional resources will be required if there is to be a significant increase in places for science, engineering and other vocationally relevant forms of study. Furthermore, as we point out in Section 3, the supply of places must move in step with the demand for them. We cannot create more good engineers merely by supplying more engineering places: it is necessary to change attitudes as well.

1.7   These objectives need to be understood and supported in the schools, which must aim to increase the number of candidates for higher education with qualifications which include one or more mathematical or scientific subjects. Such endeavours need the support, not just of the schools, but of society more generally: parents and employers, industrialists and politicians. One notable difference between the United Kingdom and most of our economic competitors is the extent to which many children in this country specialise before they enter higher education, and so limit their later choice of a career by decisions taken at the age of 16 or even earlier. This rigidity is undesirable, and in Section 4 we welcome, as the universities have generally done, the current AS-level proposals put forward by the Government for broadening the sixth form curriculum. School-leavers cannot be considered to be properly educated unless they have a grasp both of some of the humanities and of some of the sciences.

1.8   In Section 4 we also discuss the scope for the use of new technology in teaching and consider matters relating to the type and structure of courses. We argue against a reduction in length of the undergraduate degree course and against a change in the intensity of courses. We believe that continuing education, and especially post-experience vocational education, should now be seen as a major responsibility of the universities. Responsibility for maintaining academic standards in the universities should continue to be exercised by the universities themselves and in Section 6 we review current practice and suggest where improvements can be made.

1.9   University research is an important national resource on which depends much of our future scientific and technological development, and our capacity to compete internationally. The distinctive feature of the university sector is that it combines research and scholarship with teaching. Only institutions with a substantial commitment to research as well as teaching should be on the UGC's grant list. The research capability of the universities has been seriously eroded in recent years by inadequate funding through the UGC side of the dual support system and by a decline in the number of postgraduate research studentships. In Section 5 we argue that research activity needs to be increased and that this cannot be achieved by shifting resources from teaching. We propose to adopt a more selective approach in the allocation of research support among universities in order to ensure that resources for research are used to the best advantage.

1.10   At the heart of teaching and research is the quality of the academic staff. It is essential to maintain the flow of new entrants and correct the present imbalance in staffing, but to do so a minimum annual recruitment level of 3.5 per cent of the total number of staff is required. This would imply 900 or so new appointments a year and in Section 7 we discuss steps which would make this possible. We recognise the vital contribution of the non-academic staff and draw attention to a number of problems in the field of salaries and wages.

1.11   In Section 8 we discuss the severe consequences for the universities of the lower levels of funding suggested in the Secretary of State's letter of 1 September 1983. We point out that these lower levels have effectively been built into the Government's medium-term financial plans. At these funding levels national needs as we perceive them could not be met. We recommend a period of truly level funding for the recurrent grant, with additions for particular purposes, and with a substantial increase in the equipment grant.

1.12   The financing of the universities is the responsibility of Government and cannot be shifted elsewhere except in minor ways. We would wish universities to do even more than at present to seek funds from outside sources, particularly for research and consultancy. These would only supplement Government funds, not replace them. We recommend in Section 9 that the concept of deficiency funding for universities should be abandoned and that changes in the tax laws should be considered.

1.13   In Section 10 we discuss the problem of rationalisation of small departments, and propose that universities should review their machinery of government. We emphasise the leadership required of the Vice-Chancellor, and the responsibility of the Council (Court in Scotland) to ensure that hard decisions are faced.

1.14   The UGC system has generally worked well as a buffer between the universities and the Government over the past 65 years, though there have been obvious strains in recent times of retrenchment. In Section 11 we recommend that it should continue and that coordination with the public sector should be achieved by cooperation between existing bodies. But the relationship between the universities and Government has changed in the last few years; and what the Committee does and how it operates must change accordingly. Its secretariat will need to be strengthened and its facilities improved for this purpose; and it will need closer relations with a number of other bodies, particularly with the Committee of Vice-Chancellors and Principals and with individual universities.

Section 2

Student numbers

2.1 In April 1983 the DES published projections of demand for higher education in Great Britain up to the end of the century. As with earlier DES projections, there was little indication of how these had been derived; but, whereas the earlier projections had been received without demur, the 1983 projections attracted considerable criticism.

2.2 A few weeks later the Royal Society published its own projections on future university candidates in the United Kingdom. By the end of the year two projections for universities in Great Britain had been produced by the Association of University Teachers (AUT) and one by the Committee of Vice-Chancellors and Principals (CVCP). Projections for Scotland were produced by the Scottish Education Department (SED) and by the AUT (Scotland). In April 1984 a working party of the Royal Statistical Society produced a critique of these projections, with a list of recommendations and a forecast of their own. In July 1984 the DES published two alternative revised projections called Variants X and Y in *Demand for higher education in Great Britain 1984-2000* (DES Report on Education Number 100). This was followed, too late for the Committee to consider it, by a technical report on how the revised projections were derived. It is unlikely that the debate will come to an end thereby, nor in our opinion should it. That does not excuse us from drawing what conclusions we can at this stage.

2.3 We give a detailed commentary on the various projections in Annex D. Our conclusions may be briefly summarised as follows. There are good reasons not to take account of projections other than the DES 1984, the Royal Society and the first AUT projections. The Royal Society projection and the first AUT projection, both of which relate to university entrants, are derived from the same model and from almost the same data. The DES 1984 projections are for higher education as a whole; they are based on a different model and on different data. All these projections had to make use of inadequate or suspect data, because satisfactory data are not available. However, the trends that they show are essentially the same.

Home initial entrants to full-time and sandwich courses

2.4 The majority of home initial entrants are young students, ie those aged 20 or under on entry. It is on these students that the debate has concentrated. There are two main reasons for the differences between Variants X and Y in the DES 1984 projections. One is that they make different assumptions as to the rate at which demand from women for entry into higher education will catch up with demand from men. The other, which accounts for most of the difference during the present decade, is that Variant X is based on the qualified participation index (QPI)* for young home students in 1981, whereas Variant Y is based on the index for 1983. The drop in the QPI between these two years is somewhat mysterious, and the choice between Variant X and Variant Y largely depends on how it is to be interpreted. It may reflect a genuine weakening of demand; but it may be caused by a shortage of university places, even though there are unfilled places in the public sector. There is evidence, albeit inconclusive, that there is a substantial number of school-leavers who narrowly missed a university place and were unwilling to enter a public sector institution instead. Presumably this reflects the fact that the A-levels they obtained would have ensured university places two or three years earlier. If this is the case, as we believe, then it would not have helped to provide more places in the public sector; but both in 1982 and in 1983 up to 11,000 more places in universities could have been filled without any creaming off from the public sector. Whether these school-leavers represent unsatisfied demand is a question of semantics; after all, they could have entered public sector higher education had they been willing. But we believe that the existence of a substantial group of school-leavers, not quite well enough qualified to obtain university places but unwilling to enter the public sector, is a temporary phenomenon. If this is so, then in a few years' time Variant X will be a better measure of demand than Variant Y.

2.5 Scottish school-leavers choose, in the main, to seek places in the Scottish higher education system. This means that, for young home students at least, it is essential to have separate projections for Scotland; and it would be unwise to assume that trends in Scotland are the same as those for Great Britain as a whole. The projections which have been produced by the SED and by the AUT (Scotland)

---

*The QPI is defined as the number of home initial entrants aged 20 and under to full-time and sandwich higher education in a given year divided by the number leaving schools and further education establishments in the previous academic year with at least two GCE A-levels (three SCE Highers in Scotland).

do not take account of all the factors in the DES 1984 projections and are not therefore entirely comparable.

2.6 Northern Ireland school-children take A-levels which are interchangeable with those in England and Wales. The latest Northern Ireland projection suggests a smaller and rather later decline in numbers than in England and Wales. In the continuing absence of any significant influx of students to Northern Ireland from other parts of the United Kingdom it is important to the Northern Ireland economy to maintain an adequate supply of able graduates. This supply is put at risk if an increasing proportion of well-qualified school-leavers is forced to seek higher education in Great Britain.

2.7 For home students aged 21 and over on entry, the assumptions in the DES 1983 projections were much criticised, though the critics produced no competing projections themselves. The 1984 projections show a considerable change in methodology, and we regard the present model as more appropriate. The numbers projected have also increased substantially. However, demand from mature students is likely to be highly sensitive to even small changes in Government policy or in employment prospects.

2.8 For the reasons given in para 2.4 we consider that Variant X for home initial entrants should be used as the basis for planning for the latter part of this decade. However there are too many uncertainties to justify the use of Variant X to make plans now for the 1990s. First, changes in secondary schooling and examinations can be expected to improve educational attainments and, together with changes in the economic and social climate, should stimulate demand. Second, there is the question whether the number of graduates who will be produced if these projections are realised will be sufficient to meet national need.

2.9 This latter question is difficult to answer. It is impossible to apply detailed manpower planning to higher education except perhaps in a few areas like medicine and teacher training. One reason for this is that the time-scale involved is long: it takes five or six years from a school-child's choice of A-levels to graduation, whereas a manpower shortage in a particular area is seldom if ever identified until it is urgent. A more important reason is that higher education is not primarily or solely training in a narrow professional skill: it provides a broad background which enables graduates throughout their careers to acquire new skills as and when they need them. Many employers look for graduates almost regardless of the subject of their degree, provided that they are numerate and can express themselves well both orally and in writing. Even employers who look for degrees in particular subjects recognise that they have subsequently to provide training in specific skills. **As the country moves out of recession, the demand for graduates will increase across the board,** with serious effects in areas such as information technology where there is already a shortage. **Demand will not diminish in the early 1990s just because there are fewer 18 year olds available to meet it.**

Home postgraduates 2.10 We do not accept the assumption made by the DES for their 1984 projections that the ratio of home postgraduates to undergraduates will not change. Postgraduates numbers are a matter for policy rather than projection. The majority of postgraduate courses are related to employment. They variously aim for vocational qualifications, give research training and provide conversion courses and intensive instruction in specialised (and usually applied) areas of science and technology. In paras 5.22–24 we make the case for increasing the number of research students in the context of the universities' responsibilities in research: we would want to see a progressive rise from the present level of some 14,000 full-time students to about 16,000. We also see an expanding need for taught postgraduate courses in view of the increasing level of skill required in all employments. Planning should be based on rising participation, by graduates through initial professional training and by experienced professionals through continuing education. A rise from 17,000 to 20,000 full-time home students would be appropriate, with a commensurate increase in part-time provision. The combined target of 36,000 full-time postgraduates in the universities should be reached by 1990–91. We foresee no lack of able students providing the arrangements for student maintenance are adequate. This is a matter which we intend to study further.

Students from abroad 2.11 Students from the European Community at present constitute a small proportion of total numbers, and for statistical purposes modest variations in their numbers do not matter. We are aware of the possibility of a substantial increase, but it is not a possibility that we would at present be justified in taking into account in our planning. In Section 9 we discuss the importance of overseas students to our higher education institutions and the universities' prospects of taking more of them. However as a working assumption we accept that the number of overseas students, including those from the European Community, in higher education will remain constant at 45,000.

Conclusions and recommendations on total numbers in higher education

2.12 In the light of the discussion above our conclusions and recommendations are as follows:—

(i) **Provision for home initial entrants over the three years 1985–86 to 1987–88 should move progressively closer to the level of demand shown in the DES 1984 Variant X, ie to about 170,000, and should be held at that level until the end of the decade.**

(ii) **Full-time home postgraduates in the universities should be enabled to rise from about 31,000 in 1983–84 to about 36,000 by the end of the decade; of these 16,000 should be research students and 20,000 on taught courses.**

(iii) **Taking (i) and (ii) together and allowing for students from abroad, including those from the European Community, numbers in higher education should rise to about 600,000 full-time and sandwich students in Great Britain as shown in the graph below.**

(iv) **Neither the Variant X nor the Variant Y projection is reliable for the longer term. In order to provide a sounder basis for planning for the 1990s the projections should be reconsidered and recalculated in three or four years' time. On that occasion separate projections based on the same principles should be made for Scotland.**

(v) **Efforts should be made meanwhile to improve the coverage and quality of the data used for the projections.**

When the Government has decided on the total number of students in higher education, we would expect it to consult us and other bodies concerned before deciding how the places should be divided between the universities and the public sector.

Higher education (Great Britain): total full-time and sandwich student numbers

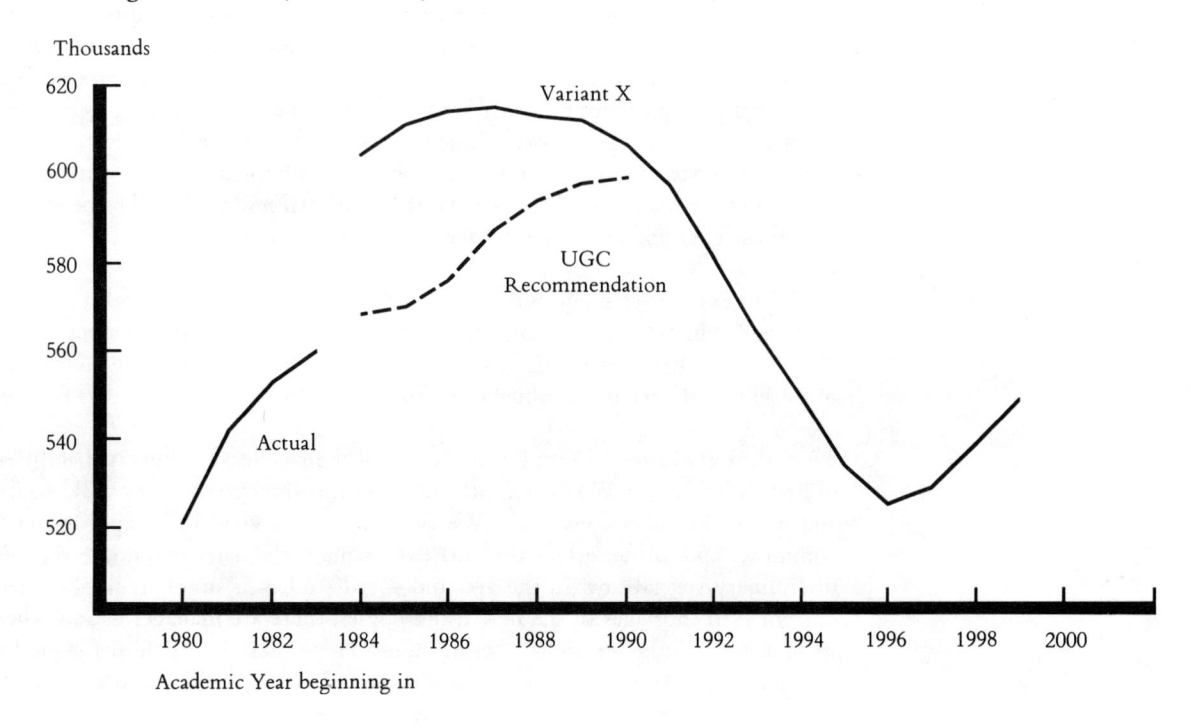

Section 3
Subject balance and the shift to Science and Technology

3.1 The Committee's plans for 1981 to 1984 provided for a shift in the science : arts ratio from approximate parity in 1979–80 to a ratio of 52 : 48 in favour of science in 1983–84. This will have been achieved not by any absolute increase in science and technology numbers but by a reduction in the number of students in the arts and social sciences. However, the additional students whom universities will be admitting in the next two years in response to a request from the Secretary of State will be largely in science and technology. The Secretary of State has asked for our advice on how universities could contribute to a further shift towards "technological, scientific and engineering courses and to other vocationally relevant forms of study" and on how large a movement might be practicable or desirable.

3.2 Between 1980–81 and 1982–83 about 60 per cent of all first degree graduates entering home employment on graduation went into industry and commerce. For students in engineering and technology, the figure was about 90 per cent; in biological and physical sciences, over 70 per cent; in social, administrative and business studies, just under 70 per cent; and in arts (language, literature, area studies and other arts), about 55 per cent. We recognise that more graduates in technological subjects are required to meet the needs of new industries and of a changing society which we have already referred to. Shortages are already apparent, most notably in electronic engineering and information technology and in some aspects of manufacturing and production engineering. In other areas of science and technology the need may be not so much for more graduates as for a better supply of graduates of the highest quality. We cannot by ourselves quantify these needs nor conclude what increase in supply is required. We understand that the Government is seeking to identify the manpower shortages more closely with a view to proposing measures to improve supply.

3.3 Universities have already run down academic staff and funding in all departments to cope with the 1981–84 cuts. In many computer science and engineering departments, for example, teaching loads are now too high and the levels of funding too low. A further expansion of places in these departments can be achieved only if additional staff are recruited. In view of the current shortage of suitably qualified people, the universities may need to look to industry to second staff. Equipment will also be needed and here too industry may be able to help, particularly if tax disincentives are removed (see para 9.10). Within the universities the resources to pay staff and to purchase and make use of equipment cannot be transferred from subject areas outside science and technology, except on an unacceptably long time-scale. Such a transfer would be from less to more expensive areas of provision, so that the addition of two science or technology places would entail the loss of between three and four arts or social science places. Additional resources will be needed if a significant number of extra science and technology places are to be provided.

3.4 Past experience suggests that supplying places is unlikely in itself to lead to a matching increase in student demand — particularly from the best students, who are the ones most desired by employers. It is not enough, therefore, simply to provide extra places. If they are all to be filled, students' choice of subjects will need to be influenced: this is best done by market signals from employers and others.

3.5 Most graduates are employed because of their general intellectual abilities. The Confederation of British Industry (CBI) has recently advised Ministers that industry will continue to need generalists and non-technical professionals. We agree with this view in its application both to industry and commerce and to the service sector. At the same time many jobs do need graduates with particular disciplinary specialisms: in the arts and social studies as much as in the sciences. Apart from the current skill shortages in the new technologies, there are managerial and other needs to be satisfied in industry, commerce and the professions. These include the need for graduates who understand foreign languages and societies, who are able to help solve the social and economic problems of our age, and who are capable of teaching the rising generation.

3.6 If employers in industry and commerce place a premium on recruits from the universities with particular qualities and qualifications, they should demonstrate this in their policies and actions, including the provision of training places for sandwich course students and new graduates. In general, industry needs to improve its image with students and, in particular, employers should make full use of the market mechanisms which are available to them, notably salary levels. Too often in the past the messages which industry has conveyed to young people in school have been muted and ambiguous.

3.7 Messages from industry are only one influence: there are forces just as powerful within the schools. The subject which a student reads at university depends on a series of decisions, each one of which narrows his options. These decisions are mostly taken between the ages of 14 and 18: in England, Wales and Northern Ireland the most critical of these is the choice of A-levels. By this choice a student will either aim towards a technological, scientific or engineering course at university or virtually rule out the possibility of such a course. On the whole, forces within the schools tend to work against the sciences, particularly for girls. This is not intended as a criticism of the schools. The attitudes which they engender to science and technology and to employment in industry and commerce reflect those in our society. If we undervalue the industrial scientist or engineer, so will our children.

3.8 In the schools good teaching of mathematics and the natural sciences is vital. Improved facilities and teachers with better training and motivation are needed in primary as well as in secondary schools. Information and advice to school-children on choice of subjects for further study, related to career aspirations, are also crucial. Schools should emphasise the importance of a balanced curriculum and should avoid the dangers of specialisation at too early an age. **If more girls could be persuaded to develop an interest in mathematics and physical sciences, the situation could be transformed.**

3.9 Because it may be necessary to increase the number of graduates in some subject areas faster than the normal market mechanisms will allow, we sought universities' views on the feasibility of conversion courses to enable school-leavers with high attainment in arts subjects to qualify for university courses in sciences or engineering. The response was that the interest in such courses was very limited, and their provision would be unlikely to increase significantly the number of first-class scientists and engineers. Where students do choose to change direction, there is already provision for this in the further education system. Most of our respondents considered that to be the most appropriate recourse. Conversion at postgraduate level is another matter. A large number of taught master's degrees provide vocationally oriented education for graduates from all disciplines, and recently there has been a large-scale development of conversion courses in information technology. The potential is great, and is limited not by demand but by the financial support available to postgraduate students.

3.10 **To summarise, our answer to the Secretary of State is that we accept the case for a further shift towards science and engineering and other vocationally relevant forms of study. It cannot, however, be pushed ahead faster than the supply of good students in the right subject areas; and it must take account of developments across the full range of the employment market. A significant increase in the number of places in science and technology can only be provided if the necessary resources are made available. Those resources cannot be found within the financial provision indicated in the Secretary of State's letter of 1 September 1983; in particular it is neither desirable nor feasible to find them at the expense of the arts.**

Section 4
Teaching

4.1 The Secretary of State has asked us, in the context of the maintenance or improvement of quality through the more efficient use of resources, to consider questions about the teaching function: the length and intensity of the courses; the balance between undergraduate, taught postgraduate and research provision; the balance between initial and post-experience education; and new approaches to teaching and learning. These questions cannot properly be addressed without regard to the attainment and potential of entrants to the universities. We therefore start by considering desirable directions of change in the school curriculum, especially in England and Wales*. **In particular we believe that school-leavers today can be regarded as having a balanced education only if they have followed courses in both arts and sciences throughout their secondary schooling.**

4.2 During the last two decades the schools have placed increasing emphasis on broadening the whole basis of the education of the adolescent; but universities, through their admissions policies and their responses to formal proposals for examination reforms, have helped to maintain a degree of specialisation in the sixth form in England and Wales which in our view has not been to the advantage of most students. We therefore welcome the proposals by the Secretaries of State for Education and Science and for Wales for AS-level examination courses to supplement and broaden the curriculum of A-level students, while at the same time maintaining academic standards *(AS levels: proposals by the Secretaries of State for Education and Science and Wales for a broader curriculum for A-level students,* DES/Welsh Office, May 1984).

4.3 The universities' attitude to this attempt to broaden the sixth form curriculum in England and Wales will be of crucial importance. We hope that they will welcome what is essentially a development of the 1980 I-level proposals which were generally endorsed by the Standing Conference on University Entrance. Opinion may, however, be divided over whether the aim should be to reduce the degree of specialisation for all pupils, or simply to make a broader sixth form education available to those who prefer it. We ourselves are convinced that the goal should be a broader sixth form education for all: indeed we hope that the present proposals will be only a first step. It will be necessary for universities to modify their entrance requirements and for departmental admissions policies to give positive weight to applicants with a broader range of subjects. Only such a step will encourage schools and students to take on the additional work involved. **Universities have a responsibility to give a positive lead in this way, and so make possible a change in the pattern of sixth form education which is long overdue.**

4.4 Much detailed work remains to be done on the precise structure of the broader curriculum, and this must take account of the resource implications for schools. Proposals like those in the consultative paper on AS-levels are unlikely to harm the standard of university education because the intention is that in their main subjects candidates will continue to reach the standard of the existing A-level examinations. However it is important that a positive move is made to reform the present highly fragmented public examination structure and to establish core syllabuses in key subjects. Universities will need to review the design and content of their degree courses, but **we believe that a broadening of the sixth form curriculum on the lines being proposed would not require a general shift to four year degrees.**

4.5 In Scotland the school curriculum has traditionally had the advantage of breadth. Although major developments are in train following the publication of *16s–18s in Scotland — An Action Plan* (SED, January 1983), the SCE Higher Grade will remain the basis for university entry. This implies the continuation and support of the Scottish three year (ordinary) and four year (honours) degree structure.

The structure of first degrees

4.6 The overwhelming consensus of our respondents was against changes in the structure of first degrees. The three year degree course is considered to be the minimum necessary to allow students to do full justice to their subjects, and to acquire the skills and develop the maturity of judgement expected of a university graduate. It is already short in comparison with European and American

---

*In the aspects which concern us in this section, arrangements in Northern Ireland are on a par with those in England and Wales, and the aim will be to maintain comparable standards. The proposals by the Secretaries of State referred to in paras 4.2–4.4 have been endorsed by the Government in relation to Northern Ireland. We refer to Scotland in para 4.5.

first degrees and it compares favourably with them in cost per graduate. To reduce the length of the standard degree course would undermine the standing of British graduates abroad. It would run counter to the trend over the last few years to lengthen some courses (eg in engineering) and would make it more difficult to introduce a less specialised sixth form curriculum. A two year self-contained course would be welcomed by some of our respondents, but only if the normal pattern was for students to take two such courses consecutively, ie to spend four years at university. Most respondents ruled out that prospect on financial grounds and stated their firm opposition to two year courses leading to a degree.

4.7 **We agree that the three year degree course cannot be shortened.** However, within the general three year format we recognise that new needs may require new structures such as modular courses and arrangements for credit transfer. We also acknowledge the value of having courses of different types and lengths within the total spectrum of higher education provision.

4.8 We do not advocate a change in the intensity of courses. In some subjects like medicine and dentistry, teaching is conducted throughout the year, and this is reflected in their more favourable staff : student ratios and higher costs. In other subjects vacation courses, field work and industrial or professional experience are required. In all subjects undergraduate students are expected to spend some part of their vacations reading and consolidating their term-time work. Research degree programmes are a twelve-months-per-year commitment for staff and students alike, as are the majority of taught master's courses. It is during the undergraduate student vacations that academic staff are able to do most of their research, develop their contacts with industry and fellow research workers at home and overseas, and prepare new courses and bring existing courses up to date. Extensive use is made of university facilities for vacation conferences, short courses and summer schools. This is a valuable source of income which universities use to keep residence charges down to levels which students can afford.

4.9 A significant minority of universities is firmly committed to sandwich courses, which are held in high regard by industry. This mode of provision is very valuable in some subjects. Its success does, however, depend on the availability of sufficient good industrial and commercial placements. We are aware of difficulties in this respect, particularly in a time of economic recession when firms tend to reduce their training places.

Continuing education

4.10 The expansion of university education in the 1960s and 1970s was concentrated mainly on the provision of full-time courses for school-leavers. Universities have, however, always had some involvement in continuing education and many have recently sought to develop their provision for mature students, for part-time study, and for post-experience vocational education (PEVE). We set up a Working Party to examine needs in this area and earlier this year it made its report. It attached particular importance to the effectiveness of continuing education, and especially PEVE, as a medium for the dissemination to key sectors of industry, commerce and the public services of new knowledge arising from research.

4.11 We are still considering the detailed recommendations of the Working Party, including those on funding. **We agree strongly with its general conclusion that continuing education in its various forms should now be seen as a major responsibility of the universities along with their responsibilities for teaching full-time students and for research.** That does not mean that the commitment of all universities should be the same. The scope for development must vary with location and with markets for vocational courses. Account must also be taken of the role of other providers, with the emphasis at local level on collaboration between universities and public sector institutions to avoid wasteful duplication. At present the development required is severely inhibited by lack of resources. There is a strong economic case for providing a financial stimulus. Universities can and should do much more to facilitate technology transfer by providing courses tailored to industry's requirements. With their strong research base, they have the potential for making a contribution of distinctive quality in continuing education.

The use of technology for teaching

4.12 The advance of technology brings new opportunities for increasing the effectiveness of teaching. Developments in information technology and distance learning will considerably extend universities' access to knowledge. Lectures recorded on video-tape can be made available to other universities and groups of students. In particular, the use of the computer in teaching and learning has exciting possibilities which extend across the whole range of disciplines, as the recent report published by the Computer Board bears witness *(Report of a Working Party on Computer facilities for teaching in universities,* December 1983). It is clear that more equipment must be provided to satisfy the demands of the greatly increased numbers of users who will require access to computing facilities. This will involve the provision of intelligent workstations and fast and reliable networking systems. A programme of education and training, to develop computer awareness for staff as well as students, is urgently required. Above all, there is the need for skilled staff in the universities to develop the basic software tools and assist in the preparation of teaching applications packages. Without these facilities the universities will fail to meet the reasonable expectations of students who will already have experienced the usefulness of computers at school, and they will not be able to produce graduates with the skills and competence that are necessary for working and living in a modern technological society.

4.13 There is, then, a pressing need for resources for the modernisation of universities' teaching methods, just as there is for the resources to modernise their estate and equipment. Past experience strongly suggests, however, that **the machine cannot replace the teacher**. His role will continue to be fundamental. New technology should not be seen as a means of reducing teaching costs significantly. What may be expected, however, is that if the capital investment in new technology is made, resources will be used more effectively to improve the quality of teaching and to extend the scope and variety of what is taught.

Section 5

Research

5.1 The Secretary of State has sought our advice on the following questions:

(i) what measures might be taken to increase the resources devoted to fundamental scientific research and to applied research and development and to encourage their most effective use;

(ii) whether greater selectivity in the funding of research activity both within and between institutions is necessary; and in particular

(iii) whether the contribution through recurrent grant to the "dual support" system should be based on greater specificity of funding, possibly involving recognition of universities' differential success in securing research monies from outside; whether coordination with the Research Councils should be stepped up and whether some funds should be allocated only after joint consideration with the Research Councils of individual universities' research plans.

5.2 Universities have a fundamental and substantial commitment to the advancement of knowledge through research and scholarship, and the quality of their research is held in high international esteem. Their ability to sustain that commitment has, however, been eroded by the progressive squeeze on their funding, culminating in the contraction in resources since 1981. We argue in this section that research is vital to the nation's future well-being, and that the universities must be given the resources to sustain their contribution to the total effort. At the same time we must ensure that those resources are put to the best possible use. **We therefore intend to develop a more systematic and selective approach to our allocation of funds for research. This will not be effective unless the universities make a complementary effort to develop explicit research strategies and improve their management.**

The present scale of research effort

5.3 The quantity of research undertaken nationally cannot be measured in the same easy way as the number of students. The best available indication is the amount of expenditure. According to the Department of Trade and Industry (DTI) the total national expenditure on scientific basic and applied research and development in 1981 was about £6,000 million; about half of this was Government-financed (*Research and Development in the United Kingdom in 1981*, an article in Economic Trends, August 1984).

5.4 University research is financed through the "dual support" system. Some funding is provided from general university income (mainly UGC grant and student fees) and some from external sources. The Research Councils collectively are the most important external source but income from charitable foundations and industry is growing fast. The major problem in attempting to quantify the cost of university research is that teaching and research are so closely interrelated that expenditure cannot be clearly divided between them. The same academic staff teach and do research, and the same accommodation, equipment and supporting staff often serve both purposes. In a sense which the refining and chemicals industries would understand, a university's outputs of research on the one hand and of graduates and postgraduates on the other may be considered as "joint products". Their separate production costs cannot be isolated, but the aggregate cost is considerably less than would be the cost of producing both separately. Nevertheless, a notional apportionment of expenditure on research from general university funds can be made on certain assumptions, one of which is that on average 30 per cent of academic staff time is devoted to research (see paras 8.27–28). On those assumptions, expenditure on university research in the United Kingdom in the financial year 1982–83 from general university funds is estimated to have been £635 million. External funding amounted to £263 million (not including Research Council support for postgraduate training) in the same year. These figures include research in the social sciences and humanities. If these subject groups are excluded the figures would be about £470 million for expenditure from general university funds and £230 million from external funding. On the basis of our estimates and of data in the DTI article referred to in para 5.3, **the universities carry out more than half of the nation's basic research**.

The national need for research

5.5 The evolution of academic disciplines and the growth of knowledge are continually offering fresh openings for research, and there are wider national needs and aspirations to be met. Whether the present level of national investment in research is adequate is a matter of judgement. However, several things can be said with certainty. First, basic research of high quality, conducted on a broad front, is a necessary condition for the emergence and exploitation of the new technologies that will be of such importance to the nation's future prosperity. Second, the cost of basic research is small compared with the cost of applied research and development. Third, because basic research takes time to work through to industrial applications, the damage caused by under-investment will not show itself at once, but eventually it will reduce the nation's ability to remain at the forefront of technical innovation. It will also delay the solution of complex problems which depend on the interpretation and integration of the findings of fundamental research in several different disciplines. Finally, the level of research activity determines whether this country retains effective membership of the international scientific community.

The need for university research

5.6 The question "How much research is needed in universities?" must be considered on its own merits. It cannot be answered simply by reference to the number of students to be taught (which depends on student demand) or to the number of staff employed to teach them (for although all the staff should have the opportunity to do research, they need not all be engaged in research to the same extent).

5.7 In basic research, as we have shown in para 5.4, the universities play the leading part. In the natural sciences and engineering, though much applied work is carried out in specialised research institutes or industry, its roots can almost always be traced to basic research carried out in universities. The practical applications of academic research which have transformed our society are well illustrated in the CVCP's report *Research in universities* of July 1980, from which we quote:

> "Many mathematical techniques which seemed esoteric and academic at the time have later proved to be of crucial value for solving problems in engineering. Fundamental studies in solid state physics in universities pointed the way to the development of the whole of the micro-electronics industry which is expanding so rapidly today. The discovery of the genetic code in a Medical Research Council unit in Cambridge University has opened up the possibility of a major new industry concerned with biotechnology. The whole organic chemicals industry, including the synthesis of dyes, drugs and pharmaceuticals, pesticides and many other chemical preparations we now take for granted, has its roots in fundamental studies by organic chemists, mainly in universities, of the structures of the molecules of natural materials and of methods of synthesising them. The fundamental work on polymerisation and the properties of macro-molecules by Staudinger which eventually led to the polymer industry we have today was started in a university laboratory. The powerful physical analytical techniques such as X-ray crystallography, spectroscopy, mass spectrometry and nuclear magnetic resonance which are now indispensable tools in most large industrial research and development laboratories were all developed from academic and basic research programmes, mainly in universities; and the universities of the United Kingdom have played a very prominent role in all these developments."

5.8 There are many advantages in locating research in universities. First, they offer the best setting for inter-disciplinary and multi-disciplinary research, because they cover a far wider range of subjects than do other research establishments. This range also facilitates shifts of research, whereas specialised institutes can be left without a useful role as knowledge advances. Second, the findings of university staff are usually disseminated rapidly to a wide variety of users and, unlike some comparable work undertaken in Government departments, have the advantage of being subjected to competitive criticism from other research workers. Third, it is well established that the research ability of staff varies throughout their career, and may tail off as they grow older. In universities this does not usually cause a problem because academic staff can take on more teaching as they do less research. Fourth, the fullest possible use can be made of library and other facilities because they are needed for both teaching and research. Finally, the close association of teaching and research gives a special strength and vitality to the universities. Able young people receive a unique stimulus from being taught by those engaged in extending the frontiers of their disciplines.

5.9 The judgement of the Committee and of the Advisory Board for the Research Councils (ABRC) is that the universities' research efforts in science, engineering and social sciences fall short of the level required for the technological, industrial and social changes which we face as we approach the end of the millennium. Specific initiatives like the Alvey programme and our own support for biotechnology show that the exploitation of the intellectual capital of the universities is a precondition for industrial regeneration. The ACARD/ABRC report (*Improving research links between higher education and industry*, HMSO, June 1983) calls for greater academic-industrial collaboration, and proposes specific measures to encourage it. **We strongly support that call, but effective collaboration in applied research must be based on a firm groundwork of basic scientific research.**

The present situation of university research

5.10 The research capability of the universities depends upon the adequacy of funding through the dual support system, the merits of which are well described in the Merrison Report (ABRC & UGC, *Report of a joint working party on the support of university scientific research*, Cmnd 8567, June 1982). Almost all our respondents agreed with Merrison's conclusion that it is the best system available for the support of university research.

5.11 The Merrison Report drew attention, however, to the deficiencies that had developed as a consequence of inadequate UGC funding. A situation which Merrison regarded as grave before the cuts in 1981 has deteriorated further. Research has suffered because there are fewer academic staff and those who remain have increased demands placed upon them. This has been exacerbated by the curtailment of facilities and support, including expenditure on libraries, computer centres and other central services, and by the inadequacy of the equipment grant. **If universities cannot provide the opportunities and facilities for research, they will not attract or retain the best minds.**

5.12 The Research Councils cannot make good these deficiencies, even if it were appropriate for them to do so. Although the Science Budget has received relatively favourable treatment, there is a growing proportion of research grant applications which the Research Councils have judged to be of the highest merit but which they have not been able to support. These problems are described in the report, which is soon to be published, of a Science and Engineering Research Council study group under the chairmanship of Sir Jack Lewis. It concludes that the ability of the academic community in the United Kingdom to undertake fundamental research to international standards is being seriously damaged. This is a matter for the gravest concern.

5.13 The Merrison Report proposed as a long-term objective that universities should channel proportionately more of their funds into research. Foreseeing that the 1981 cuts were likely to produce the opposite effect, the UGC tried to protect research by indicating reduced targets for home and EC students. This approach was significantly modified as a result of the initiative from the Secretary of State last year, which led universities to offer to admit additional students without additional grant in 1984 and 1985. Student demand for higher education is expected to rise in the next few years (see Section 2). With this in prospect, we cannot propose any further shift in the balance of university activity from teaching to research. Nor can so wide a funding gap be bridged by further improvements in teaching efficiency. There must be truly level funding of recurrent grant (see para 8.6) and a substantial increase in equipment grant (see para 8.33) if expenditure on research is to grow.

Allocation and management of research resources

5.14 We acknowledge our obligation to ensure that resources for research are allocated and managed to the best advantage. We suggest the following general principles:

(i) **The UGC should be more selective in its allocation of research support among universities.**

(ii) **Each university should know what resources it is devoting to research and the distribution of these resources should be a matter for careful planning.**

(iii) **Allocation by the UGC and planning by the university should be interactive processes.**

5.15 We have in the past taken account of research achievement, but we have not previously implemented the principle of interaction or responsiveness identified at para 5.14(iii). Rational discriminaton in the application of research funds requires not only effective management and planning of research priorities by each university but also a dialogue between universities and the UGC so that we may have as full as possible a knowledge of their plans and how they are carrying them out. Such a dialogue will be an essential part of a future allocation procedure more directly responsive to the academic planning of the universities than that of recent years. We envisage that universities should spell out in some detail their plans for research, identifying the areas of investigation and, as far as possible, the sums to be spent on them: the fact that certain major resources are common to research and teaching does not mean that institutions should not make as accurate as possible an attribution of effort or use, or that they should neglect to identify those inputs — often of significant cost — which are specific to research.

5.16 We believe that each institution on our list should have a substantial commitment to research, though not equally in each field and with a change in the balance between fields over time. It is entirely proper that the active strategy of selection which we intend to adopt should be responsive to the qualities and aspirations of each institution. Within its total allocation of recurrent grant we would indicate how far we had been able to take account of its research plans. However, we do not intend to earmark a specific portion for research, with the consequent obligation to police a specified pattern of activity and expenditure. To do so would confuse our duty to allocate resources rationally with the proper management responsibility of institutions. It would also lead to intolerable accounting problems (compare para 5.4). It is of the essence of basic scientific research that its outcomes are unpredictable and that it frequently flowers in unexpected places. Its funding must therefore provide the necessary degree of flexibility. Our strategy must be consistent with the delicate balance of the dual support system. Without petrifying the system it should recognise and support quality of attainment and make it possible for new ideas to develop spontaneously to the stage where Research Council support can be successfully claimed.

5.17 The selective approach we intend to adopt will not passively reflect the Research Councils' priorities and assessments. Their support is given in response to applications for grants for particular projects, and these applications are subject to peer review. Research Councils have a great deal of information about the research standing of individual departments — at least in those subjects in which research is expensive and unlikely to be funded from other sources. They have always made this information freely available to the UGC, and for that we are grateful. We have a different role, and the tensions and differences in emphasis which inevitably arise between us are vital forces in the dual support system.

5.18 We shall need discussions with the CVCP, the ABRC and the Research Councils on how to implement the strategy outlined above. We can only adopt it if we have an adequate planning horizon (a matter discussed further in Section 8) and if our secretariat is strengthened to give us and our sub-committees the additional support we shall need. Even if these requirements are satisfied and the Committee initiates a more selective policy immediately, it will take time to move far from the existing distribution of funds between universities. This is because universities cannot quickly adjust their expenditure downwards. There would be no gain in improving research funding in some universities at the cost of financial chaos elsewhere. Thus the rate at which the UGC can move towards this new policy will depend on future levels of funding. It could be brought about more rapidly with even a modest annual increase in resources rather than level funding, and would be seriously retarded if resources were reduced.

Research in the arts

5.19 What we have said earlier about the importance of the research effort to our economic future applies to research in the social and economic as well as the natural sciences, because such research is vital to the management of technological innovation and to society's ability to understand and cope with the processes of change. It is not applicable to the same extent to research in the arts, to which we note that none of the Secretary of State's questions are directly related. **We are just as deeply concerned for the health of research in the arts as in the sciences.** Humane scholarship is a vital support of our civilisation, and of all research and scholarship it is the most confined to the universities.

5.20 Such research has traditionally been an activity for the individual scholar with access to libraries and museums and some secretarial support. Its major resource inputs — which are not negligible — are the time which academic staff and have free from teaching and other commitments to pursue their research, and the university library. Its other requirements are usually modest compared with the equipment and technical support needed in the sciences. Nevertheless, in many areas the style of research is changing. Team projects involving computation are becoming more common, particularly in language areas. Archaeology has become a high technology area, and may be followed by others.

5.21 We do not propose the creation of a research council for the humanities. The administrative apparatus required could not be justified by the budget it would administer. We believe that it is right to continue to make use of the valuable services provided by the British Academy, and **we hope that the Academy's budget will be at least maintained in real terms to permit the support of research across the areas outside the remit of the Economic and Social Research Council (ESRC).** Similarly, we intend to maintain our level of support for arts research within recurrent grant. We could not, within present funding levels, contemplate a switch from the arts to the sciences. However, selective resource allocation and effective management at the institutional level are as necessary in the humanities as in the sciences, and we intend to include the humanities in our strategy and our dialogues with the universities.

The role of the research student

5.22 There is one aspect of research which is virtually a university monopoly: the development of the scholars and research workers of the future, through the training in research methods of postgraduate research students. Good research students are an asset of great value to their departments, stimulating and challenging the research interests of the staff, and contributing practical and tutorial teaching. They include some of the most able young minds in the country, many of whom will go on to strengthen the national research base or to make a vital contribution to innovation in industry.

5.23 It is therefore a matter of great concern that the number of home postgraduate research students fell by about 15 per cent, from 16,600 in 1972-73 to 14,100 in 1982-83, while the total number of home undergraduate and postgraduate students rose by 23 per cent. In addition, the number of overseas research students fell substantially after the introduction of full cost fees: from 9,200 in 1977-78 to 6,800 in 1982-83. The fall in the number of home postgraduate students in the sciences and social studies reflects the limitation of Research Council support due to the financial constraints on the Science Budget. In the social sciences in particular, the funding of the ESRC is now inadequate to enable it to play the proper role of a Research Council in the support of research training, and the need to make short-term economies has led to an excessive reduction in the number of students supported.

5.24 Restoration of postgraduate research studentships to a healthy level would be a very rapid and cost-effective way of making good much of the erosion of the universities' research base. **We recommend that the Education Departments and the Research Councils should seek funds to reverse the decline in the number of postgraduate research studentships.**

Section 6
Academic standards

6.1   We endorse the proposition put forward in the Leverhulme Report, *Excellence in diversity* (SRHE, 1983), page 13: "Prime responsibility for standards must rest with the higher education community. Academic freedom has intrinsic value. Nevertheless, there is a legitimate external interest, and the higher education community benefits when its quality is clearly visible." We therefore welcome the establishment by the CVCP of a group under the Vice-Chancellor of Lancaster University to study universities' methods and procedures for maintaining and monitoring academic quality and standards. A code of practice on the external examiner system, prepared as the first stage of the group's work, has been circulated to universities (*The external examiner system for first degree and taught master's courses*, CVCP, April 1984). The Government has recently established a committee under Sir Norman Lindop to review procedures for the validation of degree courses in the public sector.

6.2   To maintain academic standards:

   (i)   research pursued should be of high quality;

   (ii) curricula and learning resources should be up to date;

   (iii) teaching should be conducted effectively; and

   (iv) academic awards in different institutions should reflect comparable standards of achievement.

We discuss these in turn below.

6.3   Research is highly competitive. Academics compete for resources, for the publication of the results of their work, and for promotion and other honours and distinctions. Within their universities they have to secure equipment, space, supporting staff, travel grants and study leave. Outside their universities there are both formal and informal systems of review by peer groups, for example, of applications for research grants, of papers submitted for publication and of nominations for prizes and fellowships. The peer group extends beyond the universities to other institutions of higher learning, government and industrial laboratories, libraries and museums all over the world. This competitiveness works effectively to maintain the quality of research.

6.4   There are various means by which curricula are kept up to date. The external examiner has a part to play, and we endorse the recommendation in the CVCP's code of practice that a department should discuss with him the structure of the course, the curriculum and the assessment procedures. Another and very important means is the movement of staff between institutions. We are much concerned at the limited opportunities for this at present. New ideas on curricula are also transmitted through subject associations — both the national learned societies and the smaller gatherings of academic staff in particular disciplines. Interaction with a professional body from which a department seeks accreditation for its courses is generally beneficial. In professional disciplines not subject to formal accreditation, departments may set up advisory committees of practitioners. Most universities have procedures, through boards of study and faculty boards, for the scrutiny of new curricula put forward by departments before they are approved by the Senate. These procedures may sometimes have been attenuated as the universities have expanded and as each branch of knowledge has become more and more specialised. We are convinced of the need for the systematic review of existing curricula and their teaching, particularly where few staff changes are expected. We trust that the CVCP's group will prepare guidance for universities on procedures for scrutinising new and existing curricula.

6.5   It is the responsibility of departments to monitor teaching and make sure it is effective. We believe that they increasingly appreciate this and recognise that teaching is a corporate activity and not solely the concern of the individual. It is over twenty years since the Committee first recommended organised training for newly appointed teachers. Since then initial and in-service training have greatly expanded in other branches of education, and staff appraisal has become much more searching and constructive for professional staff in many organisations. In the universities there are modest staff development programmes, and some systematic induction for new staff is now common. This is not sufficient. The need for staff development today is greater than ever, and does not relate only to new staff. We believe that further examination of this problem is required both by individual universities and by the CVCP.

6.6 The established mechanism for securing comparable standards in academic awards is the appointment of external examiners. Universities regard this as effective, and it is extremely economical. Nevertheless reasonable criticisms have been expressed, arising mainly from the variety of practice in the selection and responsibilities of external examiners and from doubts about their influence on the teaching and assessment of students. Operation of the CVCP's code of practice would, we believe, meet these criticisms.

6.7 We are not a validating agency or an examining body; but we inevitably make judgements on the quality of each university's activities in assessing the financial needs of university education and in the distribution of funds. During their visits to universities our subject sub-committees contribute to the maintenance of standards by drawing on experience gained elsewhere to suggest changes in curricula and teaching methods.

6.8 The Leverhulme Report (pp 14-15) proposed that the universities establish an academic review body; and the National Union of Students advocates national validation. No support for either proposal has been expressed by the universities, which have pointed to the considerable resources which would have to be diverted from teaching and research. We do not support these proposals either. **The universities can justify continued independence of external scrutiny, by action on the lines suggested above.**

Section 7
Staffing

A. Academic staff

7.1 The universities need a steady renewal of their academic staff to sustain their intellectual vitality and the effectiveness of their teaching and research. At present this is not possible because the staffing is out of balance.

7.2 The first imbalance is in the age structure, as illustrated below:

(i) Less than 30 per cent of all non-clinical academic staff are aged 50 or over and in a dozen institutions the figure is below 20 per cent. This is mainly the result of the contraction of the past three years: between August 1981 and March 1984 about 2,000 staff over the age of 50 took voluntary retirement. The substantial further number of voluntary retirements which is expected this September can only make things worse.

(ii) Less than 15 per cent of staff are under 35 because recruitment in the early 1980s was well below the levels of the 1970s. This has been only partially offset by the new blood scheme.

(iii) About 60 per cent of staff are aged between 35 and 49. This is the result of high recruitment in the late 1960s and early 1970s. Most of the members of this large group will not reach retirement age until the first decade of the twenty-first century.

For comparison, a university system with a balanced age structure would have about 40 per cent of staff over 50, about 20 per cent under 35 and about 40 per cent between 35 and 49.

7.3 The second imbalance is in the staffing of different subjects. There are two aspects to this. One is that, because universities have been obliged to rely heavily on voluntary early retirement over the last three years, some subjects have suffered more than others and their present staffing is often out of balance with their commitments and needs. The other aspect is that the age imbalance which we have described above affects some subjects more severely than others. Mathematics has the highest proportion of staff aged between 35 and 49, with only 20 per cent aged 50 or over. Physical sciences has a very low proportion (10 per cent) under 35. Social studies has the largest proportion under 35 (25 per cent) but the smallest over 50 (18 per cent): in effect it is following the general pattern, but a few years behind.

7.4 The problems caused by these imbalances vary with the institutions. The age imbalance is particularly great in some of the new universities which were founded in the 1960s.

7.5 The intellectual health of the universities is critically dependent on the recruitment of young lecturers. Provided the total number of staff does not fall, recruitment in the 1990s should be sufficient, because by that time those now in their late 50s will be reaching retirement age. In the 1980s, unless the number of students increases and more staff are appointed as a result, we do not expect the universities to be able to recruit more than about 700 new non-clinical academic staff a year on average. This is based on estimates of the number of staff who will be leaving university service and assumes that the total number of staff remains constant. Details of the underlying projection, which takes 1984-85 as the baseline, can be found in Annex E and the position is shown graphically below. Data for 1983 are not yet available but, as for 1982, they will reflect the increased number of retirements made necessary by the recent reductions in funding. For the next few years, we regard the level of recruitment foreseen above as inadequate and it will be even lower if university funding is cut. **We recommend that there should be a minimum annual recruitment of 3.5 per cent of the total number of academic staff. This would imply at least 900 new appointments a year.** A figure of 3.5 per cent is below the level of recuitment for a "steady state" distribution (described in Annex E) and also below the intake before the cuts of 1981. We consider in paras 7.6-14 possible ways of achieving this recruitment figure by increasing the rate at which existing staff leave or by creating additional posts.

Non-clinical academic staff leaving university service
Number of leavers in academic year: GB universities

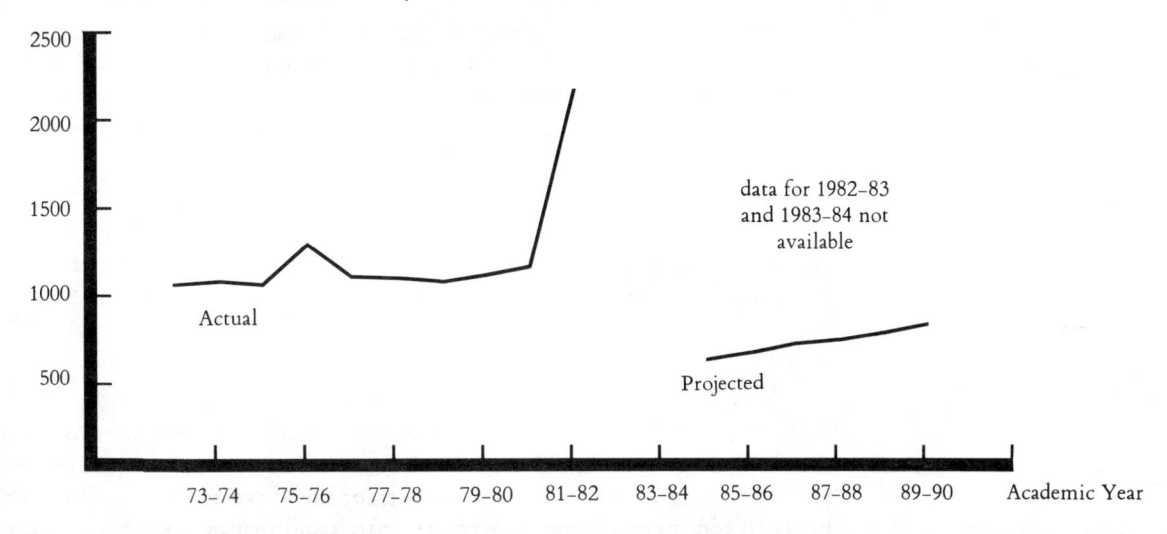

[Graph showing actual leavers from 73-74 to 81-82, rising sharply to about 2200 by 81-82; data for 1982-83 and 1983-84 not available; projected line from 85-86 to 89-90 rising from about 700 to 850. X-axis: Academic Year (73-74 to 89-90). Y-axis: 0 to 2500.]

Voluntary early retirement

7.6 In its managerial interest a university may offer early retirement to members of staff over the age of 50 who wish to go before they have acquired the maximum pension entitlement or have reached the contractual retirement age. The terms are those of the Premature Retirement Compensation Scheme (PRCS). This is a generous scheme offering up to ten additional years credit. Without it the universities could not have achieved the cuts in academic staff forced on them over the past three years. The special arrangements under which the Committee has since 1981 been able to reimburse to universities the full cost of compensation under PRCS end in September 1984. These arrangements were restricted to staff who would not be replaced.

7.7 PRCS will, of course, continue to be available to universities wishing to encourage early retirement, but the fact that from October 1984 they will have to meet the full cost from their own resources will be a strong disincentive. We see the use of PRCS as a means of creating more opportunities for the appointment of younger staff and consider that some reimbursement would be a worthwhile investment. **We recommend that the Government should make additional funds available to enable the Committee to reimburse universities with 50 per cent of the cost of compensation under the Premature Retirement Compensation Scheme.** This takes account of the fact that there would be some offsetting salary savings when staff near retirement were replaced with younger staff.

Voluntary severance

7.8 A more radical step would be to make an early and direct attack upon the problem of the unusually large 35-49 age group by continuing to offer severance terms for staff below the age of 50. We would be ready to implement this if the Government would provide the funds. However, since the terms made available in 1981-84 proved attractive to very few, considerably more generous terms would have to be offered.

Lowering the age of retirement

7.9 We estimate that if the general age of retirement was lowered to 60, either immediately or gradually, the proportion of staff leaving the system each year would increase by about one percentage point for at least the next twenty years or so. This would give a useful degree of added flexibility and it would of course be possible for members of staff still making an outstanding contribution to be re-employed after 60 on short-term contracts. However, the cost of lowering the retirement age would be considerable. The Universities' Superannuation Scheme (USS) would need to be funded to pay pensions from the age of 60, and the scheme would have to be redesigned so that staff retiring at 60 would receive at that age the pension they had expected to receive at 65. The present (tentative) USS estimate is that the cost would increase the universities' superannuation contributions by between £80 million and £90 million a year. (A more accurate calculation will be possible in the course of the 1984 valuation of the scheme.) This seems to us to rule out a general reduction in the age of retirement as a practical possibility.

Termination of appointment

7.10   In a letter to the Chairman of the CVCP the Secretary of State has recently announced the Government's objective that all universities should have the right to terminate, on grounds of redundancy or financial exigency, the appointments of all academics whose contracts were entered into after a specified date. This is an important matter on which we would wish to be consulted: we are particularly concerned that academic freedom should be safeguarded in any changes that are made. **However, any changes will have little or no effect on the universities' staffing problems over the period covered by this advice.**

7.11   More significant for this period will be the universities' ability to terminate appointments for failure adequately to perform the duties of the post. It is important that they should have an effective power to do this under the "good cause" clause of their statutes. The Secretary of State raised this matter in his letter to the Chairman of the CVCP which we referred to above. We would be prepared to comment on it if asked, but do not regard this as the appropriate place to do so.

7.12   It is equally important that universities should have the power to terminate appointments in their early stages and should exercise it effectively. In most universities the probation period is three years. This might seem to be long enough for the university to satisfy itself that the probationer is likely to continue to be productive in research and that he takes his teaching seriously and does it competently. However, if the probationer is not to have his appointment confirmed, he needs to be given warning by the end of his second year in order to have time to seek another post. The question of confirmation rightly goes to a series of academic bodies and this means that the process needs to start not later than half-way through the second year. In effect, therefore, the period during which the probationer's performance is considered is little more than a year. This is clearly unsatisfactory. **We consider that in future the probation period should be five years.**

Creation of new posts

7.13   The new blood scheme introduced in 1983 has enabled universities to recuit several hundred young academics for whom there would otherwise have been no funds. Unless it is clear that recruitment will reach 900 a year through ordinary retirements and resignations or through the possibilities which we have discussed above, we consider that some kind of new blood scheme will continue to be necessary for another four or five years.

7.14   The present scheme has been widely criticised on the grounds that, for example, it takes up far too much of the time of academics and administrators; that it pays too much regard to the research promise of groups or departments and not enough to the health of institutions; that the number of posts in the arts and social sciences is unreasonably small; that the pattern of distribution has reinforced the discrimination exercised by the Committee in its July 1981 allocations rather than assisted institutions most in need of help; that insufficient account has been taken of universities' own judgement of their most pressing needs; and that it puts undue emphasis on the new and the marginal to the neglect of vital core subjects. We have some sympathy with these criticisms and have in mind to propose a simpler scheme.

Effectiveness of existing staff

7.15   Whatever measures are taken to increase the recruitment of new staff, universities must also concern themselves with the effectiveness of existing staff. We have already discussed the need for greater emphasis on staff development in para 6.5. During the period of contraction the Committee has given some assistance with the costs of retraining and redeploying staff. There are clearly limits to what can be done: few academic staff can be expected to move from one academic discipline to another which is not closely related to it. However there can be transfers between institutions within the same discipline. We shall encourage action of this kind to promote flexibility in the use of academic staff.

7.16   Despite the increases in teaching commitments, it is important that the opportunity to take study leave should be not only safeguarded but extended. It is also important to maintain mobility within the system, so that staff may be refreshed, and their interests and outlook extended, by a change of milieu. We intend to discuss with the CVCP what might be done to encourage the movement of staff, possibly through the introduction of some sort of exchange scheme.

B. Non-Academic staff 7.17 The Committee has been impressed on its visits to universities by the loyalty and dedication of their non-academic staff, who are frequently expected to show great flexiblity in adapting to changes in working requirements and environments. Technical, secretarial and clerical staff play a vital part in the universities' teaching and research activities.

7.18 There is strong evidence that the level of technician support fell markedly during the 1970s. Although over the last three years the loss of full-time non-academic staff has been marginally less in proportion than that of academic and academic-related staff, there has also been a loss of 1,900 part-time non-academic staff (compared with 200 part-time academics). Many of the universities' responses have also dealt with the consequences of cuts in the secretarial and other support staff for the working practices of academics, who are effectively compelled to make good the deficiencies themselves. This is inefficient and wasteful. We have been told that part-time manual workers have been severely affected by cuts in hours. The workload of many of these staff, for example those concerned with the unkeep of the university estate, is not directly related to the university's teaching commitments. Contraction means that a smaller number must sustain the same burden.

7.19 The non-teaching staff unions contrast their situation unfavourably with that of their counterparts in other public services, such as local government and the health service. They contend that their earnings are lower; that they have much less opportunity for overtime or shift payments; and that they are the only major group without a national superannuation scheme. Other points repeatedly made to us on our visits to universities are the inadequacy of arrangements for induction and training, and the lack of a satisfactory career structure for the higher grades of technician. It would be inappropriate for us to pass judgement on these claims but it is necessary to draw attention to them if a balanced survey of the problems and future prospects of the universities is to be given.

C. Salaries and wages 7.20 For pay purposes university staff fall within the public sector. In each of the last few years the Government has announced a figure for the general allowance that it had made in its public expenditure plans for average increases in wages and salary bills ("the pay factor"). Although the pay factor is not a target for settlements, it is the maximum increase that can be paid without a need for offsetting savings. Pay negotiations have then established a "going rate" around which public sector pay settlements (including those to which the Government itself is a party) cluster. The "going rate" is invariably somewhat above the pay factor and indeed it is rare for any public sector pay settlement to be as low as the pay factor. In some parts of the public sector, this gap gives rise to increased expenditure; in others it is balanced by a reduction in the number of people employed. This machinery has contributed towards implementing the Government's policy of reducing numbers in the civil service. It has equally contributed to reducing the numbers employed in the university sector and the numbers supported by the Research Councils. We do not know whether these reductions are Government policy, but certainly they are direct consequences of Government policy.

7.21 Because of fundamental differences both in the machinery of pay negotiation and in the context in which negotiations take place, it is convenient to deal separately with the three groups of staff: non-academic; clinical academic; and non-clinical academic and academic-related.

7.22 Many non-academic staff in universities are on pay rates tied to those of the corresponding grade in local government. Even for those who are not, local government provides the obvious comparator, and local government pay settlements exercise a major influence on non-academic pay negotiations in universities. This is almost inevitable. In the clerical and secretarial grades, for example, local government is a major employer in most localities and a university which tried to pay below local government rates would have difficulty in recruiting satisfactory staff.

7.23 Because medical schools are integrated with selected hospitals, clinical academic staff work side by side with doctors employed by the National Health Service. There is in practice a considerable amount of interchange of duties, and indeed the system could not work as economically as it does if this were not so. Because of this, it has been accepted by the parties concerned that there should be broad comparability of remuneration between clinical academic staff and their NHS counterparts. Since salaries for the latter are determined by Government, so in effect are the former. This practice has two unfortunate consequences. First, the increase in clinical academic salaries is an increase in costs over which the universities have no control, but for which they are not fully compensated. Second, the rate of increase is normally above the "going rate" and has in recent years been well above the rate of increase in other academic salaries.

7.24 It is on non-clinical academic and academic-related pay settlements that the constraints of cash limits have borne most heavily. In each recent year settlements have been below those of the obvious comparators (academic staff in public sector higher education and administrative civil servants) and below the rate of inflation, even though they have been above the pay factor.

7.25 One reason why these relatively low settlements have been acceptable is the long incremental pay scale for lecturers. Even though pay settlements have been below the rate of inflation, a lecturer not at the top of the scale has found that his salary was rising faster than inflation because of the combined effect each year of a pay settlement and an extra increment. (This is the phenomenon of incremental drift, which is currently costing about 1 per cent a year of academic salary bills.) This does not work for lecturers at the top of the scale, and about 45 per cent of lecturers are now in that position: for this reason among others, pay negotiations are becoming more difficult each year.

7.26 Another important consequence of recent pay settlements is that academic starting salaries have depreciated, both in real terms and in comparison with outside earnings. In subjects such as electronic engineering and computing, there is already a shortage of well-qualified applicants for advertised vacancies, and this is now spreading to other subjects. In the United States the problem is even more acute: in most universities it is becoming almost impossible to maintain the quality of staff in engineering faculties against competition from industry.

7.27 The structure of the academic profession has evolved as much through chance as through design. In contrast with almost all other careers, promotion for an academic does not involve a change in the nature of his job. Readers, senior lecturers and lecturers are alike engaged in teaching and research; so largely are professors, though they also have a significant leadership and planning role. People are promoted because they do the same job better than their colleagues, and after promotion they go on doing the same job. In effect, a promotion is a merit award.

7.28 We believe that both the CVCP and the AUT, who are the two bodies primarily concerned, see advantages, as we do, in changing the academic career structure, though we do no know how far their ideas can be reconciled. Restructuring costs money. **We hope that the Government would regard the low academic pay settlements of recent years as a justification for providing the necessary money if a programme of restructuring could be agreed between the CVCP and the AUT.**

7.29 Academic pay negotiations are conducted through complicated machinery, which was necessary in the days when the Government had to be involved in the negotiations because it would have to pay the resulting bill. In conditions of cash limits, that argument no longer applies. That the present machinery works at all is a tribute to Sir Alexander Johnston, who has been Chairman of Committee A of the Universities Academic Salaries Committee since it was first established. **We recommend that the present machinery for the negotiation of non-clinical academic salaries should be reviewed.**

Section 8
Finance

8.1 Our terms of reference require us "to enquire into the financial needs of university education". It is our duty to say that these needs are:

> for recurrent grant, a period of truly level funding at least until the end of the decade (paras 8.2–17) and a longer planning horizon (paras 8.18–21);
>
> for equipment grant, an increase of at least 25 per cent (paras 8.29–33); and
>
> for capital grant, maintenance of the current level in real terms (paras 8.34–40).

Recurrent grant: level of funding

8.2 We asked universities about their plans for the rest of the decade on the assumptions of constant student numbers and constant resources in real terms. We also asked what would be the effect on those plans if income fell by either 1 per cent or 2 per cent a year but numbers were to remain constant.

8.3 The general response to the first question was that universities would as far as possible:

(i) repair the damage caused by the sudden and severe cuts imposed in 1981. In particular, they would spend more on items which, because they could be cut quickly, bore the brunt of the emergency measures necessary in 1981–82;

(ii) complete the reorganisations which were triggered off by the 1981 cuts; and

(iii) expand in selected areas, in particular postgraduate work and research, as rapidly as resources could be freed by contraction in other areas.

8.4 In answering the second question the universities made it clear that even a 1 per cent cut per year would undermine these plans. Some universities would have to shed staff because there would be insufficient retirements or resignations in the ordinary course of events. In particular it would require a virtual freeze on new academic appointments: this would have a disastrous effect on the intellectual vitality of the university system. All universities would find it difficult to respond to the appearance of new and exciting subject areas, even those likely to be of great importance to the well-being of the country. No university believed that it could secure enough additional untied income from other sources to compensate for a continued annual cut of 1 per cent. We agree with this view, for the reasons given in Section 9.

8.5 A 2 per cent cut per year would exacerbate all those effects, to such an extent that most universities were unwilling to explore its implications in detail. Broadly speaking, they said that it would force them to pursue any kind of reduction of expenditure available to them, almost irrespective of the damage it might cause to them and to the nation generally.

8.6 If the university system could be redesigned *ab initio*, no doubt it could be more economical than at present. How much more economical it could be is debateable, but that is not a profitable question to pursue. The major disadvantage of the system which we have now is that its growth was halted when many institutions were only part way to their intended size and shape. The system has been adapting itself to the cessation of growth, but radical change without growth is a difficult and complex process that takes time. Change combined with contraction cannot be achieved without substantial damage. For what governs the rate at which change can be achieved by acceptable means is the rate at which resources become free and can be redeployed. Contraction means that resources are taken away as fast as they become free: indeed, the universities very largely had to meet the 1981 cuts by mortgaging their freedom of manoeuvre for years to come. We do not believe that the universities could satisfactorily teach the present number of students with fewer resources than they now have. But it is probable that with truly level funding they would be able to teach more students than they now do, and this is significant in the light of our recommendations on student numbers in Section 2. Truly level funding here means level funding in volume terms — that is, the funding that would be needed to finance the present levels of staffing, purchase of books, periodicals, consumables, and so on. **We recommend that the Government should at a minimum provide truly level funding of recurrent grant at least until the end of the decade, which is the period for which we have made recommendations on student numbers.**

8.7 This recommendation for level funding does not cover various developments discussed elsewhere in this advice which would require additional recurrent grant: a shift in the balance of student numbers towards science and technology (Section 3); the expansion of continuing education (para 4.11); reimbursement of compensation for premature retirement (para 7.7); some form of new blood scheme (paras 7.13-14); and an industrial "seedcorn" fund (para 9.18).

8.8 For several years now the Committee has hoped, with some encouragement from the Government (eg in the 1983 Public Expenditure White Paper, Cmnd 8789), that the cuts of July 1981 would be followed by a period of level funding. It is on this basis that we have formulated our policy and our advice to universities. The Government's actions and its spending plans to 1986-87 have not borne out these hopes.

8.9 First, the universities have been hit by Government decisions which could be neither foreseen nor forestalled. For example, in July 1983 £23.5 million was clawed back from the UGC grant for 1983-84, and in the 1984 Budget VAT was imposed on building repairs. This latter decision will lead to substantially increased costs — up to about £5 million per annum by 1987-88 — and there is as yet no indication that universities will be compensated for these.

8.10 Second, apart from these haphazard cuts, the universities must expect to suffer an annual reduction of at least 1.5 per cent in volume terms. The plans in the Government's 1984 Public Expenditure White Paper (Cmnd 9143) imply an average cut in the recurrent grant of 0.5 per cent a year in real terms up to 1986-87, even assuming that the provision for pay and price increases will cover those increases. (This assumption is implicit in the use of the phrase "in real terms".) About two-thirds of the expenditure of universities is on wages and salaries, so the change in volume terms in universities' income is crucially affected by how near the actual pay increases are to the provision made by the Government. In most recent years, there has typically been a gap of at least 1.5 per cent, producing a further cut in total resources of at least 1 per cent a year. It will be asked whether that is the fault of universities as employers, or whether it is beyond their control. We have discussed this in more detail in Section 7 but the short answer is that the universities have come closer to implementing the Government's announced guidelines on public sector pay than the Government itself has done.

8.11 It is necessary to be clear what can be achieved by greater efficiency and what cannot. The Government's expenditure plans referred to above have already assumed a measure of increased economy, and we await with interest the outcome of the Jarratt Committee on efficiency studies in non-academic areas. There is also some scope for improved efficiency in academic areas, though it is important not to lose sight of the need to maintain quality and effectiveness. Improved efficiency typically makes it possible to achieve more with the same resources. It does not so easily make it possible to achieve the same results with fewer resources, because many of the assets are fixed and their scale and cost cannot be reduced quickly.

8.12 If, as we have said in para 8.10, resources continue to decline by at least 1.5 per cent a year, the total fall between now and the end of the decade will be of the same order as the 1981 cuts, although spread over a longer period. In addition there may be further irregular cuts of the kind described in para 8.9. In such circumstances, substantial damage to the system and to national interests would be unavoidable. The role of the Committee could only be one of damage limitation. It would have to advise the Secretary of State how to choose between three kinds of strategy:

(i) To let the cuts fall equally.

(ii) To distribute the cuts unequally as in 1981, though not necessarily on the same pattern as then.

(iii) To remove one or more institutions completely from the grant list.

To continue to hope that each year would be the last year in which there are cuts would be equivalent to choosing (i) should the cuts continue to occur year by year.

8.13 For a variety of reasons, the choice of strategy would have little if any effect on the number of staff that would have to be shed if there were continued cuts. First, savings through the elimination of waste have been exhaustively pursued since 1981, even where they had not been pursued before. Second, although the immediate effect of the 1981 cuts was a reduction in non-pay expenditure, this was largely because, unlike expenditure on pay, non-pay items could quickly be cut (but often only as a temporary expedient) or postponed. There is unlikely to be much scope for further significant reductions in non-pay expenditure (except possibly under strategy (iii)). In particular, even if staff numbers are reduced, it would be very difficult to achieve a corresponding reduction in the use of space. **We conclude that since pay is the dominant component of university expenditure, accounting for about two-thirds of the total, each fall of 1 per cent in the real income of the university system would mean a fall of at least 1 per cent in the number of staff employed.** No choices the Committee could make would avert this: we could only decide how the fall was to be distributed between institutions.

8.14 We consider that (i) is the least satisfactory of these three strategies. The effect on all universities would be stultifying and there would be little scope for change other than uneven and haphazard decline. The justification of the university system is quality, and (i) would involve a greater loss of quality than either (ii) or (iii). Whatever the financial constraints, this country must seek to preserve a university system which maintains international standards in teaching and research.

8.15 Severe contraction of size must carry with it comparably severe contraction of coverage. If strategy (ii) was chosen, the best way of implementing it would be as far as possible by the closure of complete departments. Some academic staff could be transferred to other universities but many more would have to retire prematurely. Substantial funds would have to be provided to meet the cost of compensation, but this would probably be true of strategy (ii) in any form.

8.16 Universities are even less well able to bear drastic cuts now that they were in 1981. There is a real possibility that strategy (ii) could not be carried through in the form described above, especially if the Government was trying to achieve a shift in subject balance as well as a general contraction. In particular, tenure would be a major obstacle. In that case we would be forced, with extreme reluctance, to recommend to the Secretary of State that strategy (iii) be pursued. If that were to be done, we would need to give advice on academic considerations, but the actual choice of the institutions to be removed from the grant list would have to be made by the Government. It is not a choice that could be made by the Committee, for two reasons. First, we could not assess the non-academic factors involved. Second, our present relationship with universities, on which our ability to do our job depends, could not survive making such a choice.

8.17 We would add that we do not clearly understand the implications of strategy (iii), either for the institutions concerned or for the Government. If an institution were removed from our grant list without being provided with any other source of public funds, it would presumably be unable to continue to function. Yet it would at the least have better qualified staff and students and better facilities than most institutions in the public sector. To let its assets go to waste in this way would be a loss to higher education and to the nation which could not be defended.

Recurrent grant: longer-term planning

8.18 To respond to changing needs in higher education, universities must keep their courses under review, developing new ones and abandoning others. They cannot do this effectively when the future is uncertain. New courses take time to plan. The entrance requirements, the curriculum, and the staffing and services must all be worked out in detail and advertised some 18 months before the course actually starts. Professional bodies may have to be consulted and their accreditation obtained. The students then take three or four years to progress through the course, which may well be revised in the light of their experience. Thus five years or more will elapse between the original idea for a new course and the graduation of the first intake. If universities cannot see some distance ahead, they are in a weak position to encourage imaginative developments.

8.19 The quinquennial system was abandoned in the early 1970s, partly because of the inflationary crisis, partly because the Government no longer felt able to commit itself for five years at a time, and partly because fewer students wanted a university education than the then financial plans had assumed. Since then the Committee has repeatedly expressed its concern about the damaging effect of the absence of a clear basis for forward planning. After the experience of recent years, the universities have little confidence that they can take at face value even the firm figures announced for the very next year, let alone the provisional figures for one or two years further ahead.

8.20 Universities must be able to plan ahead, and we need to help them to do so, in order that resources may be used effectively. It is a heavy burden for universities to prepare detailed academic plans and for the Committee to examine them. The task cannot be undertaken for the whole system more than once every three years at best. It is nevertheless vital that the system should not go for too long without the Committee making a full assessment of its policies and reviewing the distribution of resources — a much more difficult task when funds are stable or reducing than when they are increasing.

8.21 We recognise the difficulty for the Government of a financial commitment beyond its own three year planning period. Nevertheless, inflation is now lower than it has been and **we recommend that the Government should introduce a longer planning horizon for recurrent grant.** This could be achieved by a firm figure of grant for the next year (August to July) and a provisional figure for the following three academic years. The alternative of one firm figure and two provisional figures, which was adopted in 1981, is less attractive and is the minimum that would be useful. We must add that provisional planning figures are of little value unless universities can feel confident that they will be confirmed in due course. This longer horizon would also enable the capital requirements of the system to be planned in a more rational way.

Recurrent grant: the allocation process

8.22 We intend to consider changes in our approach to the distribution of resources within the university sector. These would need discussion with the CVCP and, if agreed, would take some time to introduce.

8.23 Many of our respondents felt that the Committee's present process of resource distribution had a number of shortcomings — notably that institutions did not know how the grants were determined nor what weight had been given to different aspects of institutional operations and performance; in particular, there was no indication of the proportion of the total attributable to research. Whereas the teaching demands are fairly clear, the resource requirements of research are much less readily identifiable and they are therefore vulnerable when total funds are being cut.

8.24 The Committee's present grant distribution process is primarily based on the process used under the quinquennial system. It is essentially concerned with deciding what modifications should be made to the current baseline for each institution and what additions should be made in respect of special initiatives and developments. The quinquennial system served well enough so long as resources were increasing in real terms, but strains began to appear in the 1970s. They have been increasing since 1980–81, the year in which the subsidy for overseas students started to be removed from the recurrent grant. The 1981 exercise introduced an even greater change in the distribution of resources because of the Committee's selective approach. This brought considerable criticism, but so long as there is any element of judgement involved in the grant allocation process, it is unlikely that any fully quantified explanation would be possible.

8.25 Any acceptable allocation process will have to give individual universities scope to improve their relative position, measured by the total income they are able to attract. So far as the Committee's grant to a university is concerned, two possible grounds for an increase stand out. One is that the excellence of the university's teaching or its proposals for new courses leads to a rise in the student numbers which we assume in determining our grant. The other is an improvement in the university's reputation for research.

8.26 We turn now to the issue of financial comparisons between the universities and the public sector. On teaching in particular there has been much discussion over the years about whether there are systematic funding differences between the two sectors and, if so, whether they can be explained by differences in quality, levels of work, economies of scale and so on. The DES are now attempting to produce an authoritative statement, though in our view their first version published in July 1983

(Higher education: comparisions of funding and costs across sectors) is a long way from this. Analysis of the figures is a complicated business. There is the particular difficulty that teaching and research are joint products, in the sense described in para 5.4, and the costs of joint products can only be separated in an arbitrary manner. In particular, the lack of any necessary connection between research expenditure and student numbers means that any discussion phrased in terms of unit cost or unit of resource obscures the true issues. This is not to deny that some degree of comparision is possible and it is important that the DES should continue their work, though we do not expect rapid progress. However, we believe that their aim of reducing the complex array of information about either sector to a single figure for teaching cost per arts-equivalent student is misguided and carries the risk that false conclusions will be drawn. What really matters is that in each sector the funds devoted to teaching should be fully adequate for the purpose.

8.27 Quantitative analysis of research effort in the universities is based on a survey of the use of academic staff time carried out by the CVCP in 1969–70. The broad conclusion of the survey, which relied on self assessment, was that on average academic staff spent just over 40 per cent of their working year on teaching (ie undergraduate and graduate course work), 30 per cent on research (ie personal research and the direction of graduate research), and just under 30 per cent on administrative an other activities that could not be clearly attributed to either teaching or to research. These proportions varied between subjects (being greater than 30 per cent for the experimental sciences and less than 30 per cent for other subjects), between institutions, and between different levels of academic staff. The allocation of the 30 per cent to research, and the other 70 per cent (ie including all "overheads") to teaching is an arbitrary decision. In our present state of knowledge, it would be just as plausible to derive a percentage spend on research in the university sector by assuming that the teaching cost in the two sectors were the same.

8.28 The CVCP survey is the basis of all subsequent statements about the research effort in the universities. Because it was made so long ago and because the reliability of its method of self assessment is open to question the DES have commissioned a renewed attempt to assess the distribution of expenditure between research and teaching. Preliminary results based on a pilot study in about a dozen institutions (polytechnics as well as universities) and covering about half a dozen subject groups should be available before the end of 1984. If the method seems sufficiently promising, a more comprehensive survey will be carried out.

Equipment grant 8.29 In 1978–79 DES officials accompanied our Equipment Sub-Committee on a number of visits to see for themselves the problems which universities were facing over equipment. A model for determining the level of equipment grant was then devised by DES officials in collaboration with the Committee's officers. In fact the grant has always fallen well below the figure given by the model — and we could give ample reasons why even the model itself is no longer adequate. The backlog now stands at over £380 million at current prices (see Annex F). As a consequence, there is not enough equipment available for teaching in universities and much of it is obsolete. This has been true in science, technology and medicine for some years. It is increasingly true also of the social sciences and the arts as they come to rely more and more on equipment for teaching. Updating the equipment model would raise the level of grant it would call for; but there seems little point in doing this when the actual grant is well below the figure given by the present model.

8.30 The shortage of equipment also reduces the effectiveness of the teaching of postgraduate courses, particularly information technology and other technological courses with a vocational orientation which the Government wishes the universities to expand. These subjects are developing rapidly and are suffering especially severely from obsolescent equipment.

8.31 Many departments cannot afford to purchase the modern equipment which is in general use in industry and which industrial employers expect graduates to be familiar with. Few chemistry departments, for example, can afford to equip their teaching laboratories with the full range of modern analytical chemical equipment and associated data stations now commonly used in the chemical industry. Again, the Government's policy of providing computers in schools means that undergraduates expect better access to computers at university than they did even five years ago. In the research field the case for additional funds for equipment has been strengthened by the creation of research posts in information technology as part of the IT initiative. The burden on an already inadequate equipment base is made worse by the research contracts which the Government encourages universities to accept, but which do not contain adequate provision for overheads.

8.32   The increasing sophistication of much modern equipment not only makes it more expensive to buy, but also more expensive to maintain. Whereas previous generations of equipment could often be maintained by the university itself, there now has to be greater reliance on the manufacturers, whose maintenance contracts can be costly.

8.33   The Government should accept the figures in Annex F as demonstrating the serious gap between the resources which universities require for equipment and the sums which they have been receiving. This gap will be difficult to make good. As a first step, **we recommend that the equipment grant should immediately be increased to the level indicated by the equipment grant model (that is, by at least 25 per cent) and should not again fall below it.**

Capital grant   8.34   The university estate is valued at about £7,000 million. The Committee has frequently said that it cannot be maintained in good order, still less restructured to meet changing needs, without substantial annual expenditure.

8.35   Any building eventually reaches an age at which it needs very substantial repair, and some will show weaknesses of design or construction. Many of the buildings provided in the 1960s are now reaching this stage. The Committee estimates (on the basis of a survey carried out in 1980) that universities ought to be spending at least £100 million annually on maintenance (1st quarter 1984 prices) — that is, about 1.3 per cent of capital value. Because of other claims on recurrent grant, universities are in fact spending only about £80 million annually on maintenance. This is part of our case for truly level funding for the recurrent grant.

8.36   For some buildings, however, maintenance is not enough. They need to be replaced, either because they have reached the age when they are beyond economic repair, or because they can no longer meet the changing needs of the subjects for which they were built, or because of the more stringent health and safety regulations introduced in recent years.

8.37   When, in addition, the system has to adapt to a different subject balance and lower levels of funding, major rationalisation of buildings is often unavoidable. Substantial capital funds are required for both these purposes. The Committee has a programme of about £25 million a year, split about equally between medical and non-medical building. The programme is already under severe strain. Important projects like libraries, new laboratories and technology buildings are having to be held back to allow urgent restructuring, particularly, in London, to go ahead and there is a queue stretching into the 1990s of proposals for new buildings which will be essential whatever strategy for higher education is adopted. A reasonable planning horizon and an assured level of adequate funds are essential for orderly planning. An increase in capital grant of at least 50 per cent could be easily justified but, having regard to the even more urgent needs described in this advice, **we recommend that the capital grant should be held at its current value in real terms for the next two years, but should then be sympathetically reviewed.**

8.38   In the meantime, some assistance could be provided by a more generous scheme for the retention of proceeds of sale of grant-aided property. At present universities can retain up to £100,000 of the proceeds without seeking the Committee's prior approval of the building purposes to which the sum retained would be put. Where universities wish to retain more than £100,000 the Committee's prior approval is required. Universities would like the £100,000 limit either to be raised or to be removed altogether. They would like a similar scheme for the retention of rents, which at present have to be surrendered. Finally, they would like to see some of the restrictions and limitations removed from other procedures, for example those for the provision of loans and for the use of publicly-funded assets as security for short-term bridging finance when all the proceeds are to be devoted to new work.

8.39   We support the universities in these requests, which we believe would give them much-needed flexibility in the management of their estates and enable them, and us, to make the best use of the resources already available within the system. Flexibility is a prerequisite of management. **We recommend that the retention limit of £100,000 on the proceeds of sale of property should be doubled. In circumstances where the Committee's prior approval is required universities should be allowed to retain the entire proceeds, whatever the amount.** We shall be putting forward a detailed scheme for the retention of rents.

8.40   Universities' capital assets should be managed as efficiently as possible and there should be no unnecessary restrictions on the use to which existing capital assets can be put. Universities' needs for capital grants, loans and other funds have to be considered as a whole. **We recommend that the Committee's delegated authority should be extended so that it is able to cover all aspects of universities' capital proposals.**

Section 9

Alternative sources of funding

9.1 The Secretary of State sees a reduction in the universities' dependence on public funds as important for two reasons. First, the higher the proportion of university income that comes from non-Government sources, the greater their freedom of action and their ability to survive fluctuations in the level of recurrent grant. Second, the Government intends in any case to reduce the share of the Gross Domestic Product which is devoted to public expenditure.

9.2 Until the Second World War tuition fees, endowments and local authority grants provided the greater part of universities' funding. The Government's contribution was comparatively small. This worked when the number of universities was small, with only a slow increase from 20,000 students to 50,000 over the first forty years of the century. Since the War local authorities and private donors have generously supported the foundation of new universities but Government funding on an entirely new scale has been essential. The following table shows as simply as possible the sources of universities' recurrent income in 1982-83:

£ million

"Public funding"

UGC recurrent grant	1,205
Home student fees and research training support grants	150
Research grants from Research Councils	114
Computer Board grants	16
	1,485

"Other income"

Endowments, donations and subscriptions		20
Services rendered: Overseas student fees	83	
Research grants (other than from Research Councils) and contracts	145	307
Other items, including continuing education	79	
Other sources		66
		393

9.3 We distinguish and discuss below two main types of "other income". First, there are donations, sometimes made without conditions, but more often directed towards a specific new development (eg a new building or the endowment of a Professorship, possibly for a limited period). Second, there are payments for services rendered, that is, for specific teaching or research. We must emphasise that the only part of the payments for services rendered which can be thought of as a substitute for public funding is the surplus of the payments over the cost of providing the services. Frequently there is not a surplus but a deficit. We return to this point in paras 9.15-16.

9.4 We would wish the universities to increase their "other income" and we welcome the reports of working groups of the CVCP on *Alternative funding* and of the Conference of University Administrators on *Boosting university income*, both issued in July 1984. But we must state clearly our belief that any Government which looked for a major change in the balance between public and private funding of universities would be deceiving itself. Government must ensure a "core" of public funding to provide the teaching and research which are in the national interest. Other income — even uncommitted other income — can be generated and used for valuable purposes. However, those who provide it will not expect it to be used to compensate for a failure on the part of Government to meet its responsibility to provide "core funding".

9.5 Similar views were expressed by all those of our respondents who commented on the matter. The CBI, to take one example, said:

"The state must continue to support higher education. It cannot opt out. It is unrealistic to expect anything more than marginal funding from business, which is after all only one of the users of the higher education system. Funding from that source would be likely to be specific, company oriented, largely short or medium term, subject to market fluctuations and liable to cut-off."

Donations 9.6 Whenever donations to universities in this country are discussed, unfavourable comparisons are made with the USA. It is true that gifts from corporations, foundations and alumni form a significant part of the total revenue of some American colleges — as high as 20 per cent in some exceptional cases. However, private universities benefit far more than public ones, and the scale of giving should not be exaggerated. In 1980-81 direct voluntary support represented only 6.2 per cent of total institutional expenditure (a fall from 9.5 per cent in 1965-66) and almost half of that came from individuals. There are major obstacles to reproducing American experience over here. The American tradition of substantial support by alumni is virtually unknown in this country (and in continental Europe) and cannot be established quickly; the very uneven distribution of wealth in the USA is more conducive to charitable giving; and the tax laws there provide greater encouragement to make donations.

9.7 Large donations occur relatively haphazardly, though Vice-Chancellors and other senior officers of universities put a great deal of effort into trying to secure them. Moreover they are almost always earmarked. We doubt whether there is much more that universities can usefully do to attract large donations. Any increase, particularly from companies, will depend chiefly on an improvement in the economic climate. Smaller donations, primarily from alumni, are another matter. Here we think there is scope for more initiative than most universities have so far shown. Provided the whole institution is committed to the enterprise and allocates some initial investment to set up an office and maintain an up to date register, we would expect income to start to be generated fairly quickly. However, institutions need more incentives to build upon the core funding which it must fall to Government to provide, and possible disincentives must be removed.

9.8 We already offer some incentives. For many years we have been prepared in appropriate cases to meet the cost of professional fees and furniture where money has been offered for new buildings. Two years ago we announced that universities which attracted additional income from external sources would no longer suffer a consequent reduction in grant. That is still our policy and we intend that it should remain so: we must emphasise that this represents a philosophy of core funding, not one of deficiency funding.

9.9 Under the quinquennial system the recurrent grant made available by the Government was explicitly related to planned student numbers and the funds needed to provide for them. The grant was reduced to take account of universities' "other income" over the previous five years. In other words, the grant was a deficiency grant. Today the Government determines recurrent grant largely by what it judges the country can afford. Our understanding is that it does not now take external income into account; but this is not generally known in universities. Indeed the Secretary of State seems to imply that any additional income which universities secure would lead to a lower level of recurrent grant. We can think of few stronger disincentives for industry, charitable bodies and individuals to make, or to increase, donations to universities. **We recommend that the Government should make an explicit statement revoking the principle of deficiency funding so as to encourage universities and potential donors.**

9.10 **We also recommend that the Government should consider changes in the tax laws which would help universities to raise more income.** These might include:

(i) allowing single covenanted donations to be set against tax in the year of donation, and non-convenanted gifts from individuals to be tax deductible;

(ii) relaxing some of the rules which restrict the setting of corporate gifts against corporation tax, so that, for example, donations of equipment qualify and the purpose of donations is not restricted to the general benefit of the trade or profession of the donor;

(iii) allowing all fees paid by individuals for educational courses to be tax deductible;

(iv) granting universities exemption from VAT (thereby saving direct costs and the staff expense involved in making returns); and

(v) encouraging UK based companies through tax incentives to spend more of their UK research budgets in universities.

Payment for services rendered

9.11 Payments for specific teaching and research services take three main forms: fees from overseas students; fees for other services such as continuing education courses; and research grants and contracts. We discuss these in turn below. Home student fees, most of which are paid from public funds, should not be regarded as payments for services rendered, but as part of the core funding of universities.

9.12 In 1979 the Government decided that the recurrent grant should no longer subsidise overseas students and "full cost" fees were introduced in Great Britain.* (In this context, "full cost" implied the need to replace through fees the subsidy previously given through recurrent grant.) In practice this resulted in a substantial loss of funds, the more so because, as expected, the number of entrants fell sharply in 1980–81 even though most fees charged were still below average cost. During the last four years universities have worked hard to build numbers up again, and they are now only 13 per cent below the number in 1979–80. This is a remarkable achievement and, although it has not replaced the whole of the lost funds, overseas student fees are now an important source of income for many institutions. However, there is increasing competition from subsidised institutions overseas, and at any time the supply of students from particular countries may suddenly dry up, usually for political reasons or because of fluctuations in the exchange rates.

9.13 Since the change in Government policy described above the Committee has, after consultation with the CVCP, recommended to universities minimum fees for overseas students. We are likely to continue to do this for another year or two in order to smooth the transition to a more competitive regime.

9.14 Continuing education is the second main source of "other income". Of particular interest in connection with the generation of additional income are courses of post-experience vocational education (PEVE) which are tailored to the needs of individual companies or local groups. There is a large buoyant overseas market for PEVE courses, and a considerable one also among home students despite the Government's policy that the fees for such courses should be set at a level which covers their costs. We must emphasise that this means the full costs, both direct and indirect. Courses that attract fewer students than had been planned for are likely to show a deficit. To balance this we hope that fees for PEVE courses will be set at a level which enables them, when fully-subscribed, to produce a surplus. We do not believe, however, that PEVE courses as a whole can be expected to make a significant financial contribution to the support of other university activities.

9.15 Universities carry out a great deal of non-commercial research. For some of this they are able to attract outside support from the Research Councils, from charitable bodies, and occasionally from elsewhere, though this may only meet part of the direct cost of the research. It is important to distinguish support of this kind from payments for commercial services where the university should make certain that it is not using its general income to subsidise its customers. Such payments should at the very least cover the full direct and indirect costs of providing those services. Normally there should be a surplus which could be used to support other university activities. An alternative in the case of research with commercial promise is for the university to receive an immediate payment together with a share in the potential profits which may come from exploiting the work.

9.16 Contracts which are not properly costed and which, for example, cover only the direct costs will generate additional income in the short term but will drain a university's resources in the long

---

*In Northern Ireland, where the proportion of overseas students was lower than in Great Britain, the Government did not wish for educational reasons to take steps which would further reduce that proportion. It has therefore been left to the institutions concerned to fix the level of fee to be charged for each course, but grant is determined on the assumption that the universities charge fees which at least cover the actual additional costs of providing tuition for the students concerned.

term. The Committee issued detailed guidance on costing in 1970 (published in our *Annual Survey 1969-70*, Cmnd 4593) and universities are regularly reminded of its importance. We are still not satisfied that they are obtaining the right levels of overheads on many of their research contracts and we intend to review the position. Universities must recognise that their basic functions of teaching and research may be damaged if sponsored work is subsidised from general income which is already under great pressure. Their customers must in turn be prepared to meet the full cost of the services provided for them. Government Departments in particular commonly fail to do this. **We recommend that it should be drawn to the attention of Government Departments that they should meet the full cost of the research which they commission in universities.**

9.17   We welcome the Government's decision to release universities from the obligation to work through the British Technology Group. Commercial exploitation of university research can reap rewards which are much greater than the cost of the intellectual property invested in it. Universities realise the need to preserve for themselves the right to a share in the profits from the exploitation of their research. Hitherto this has generally been done by attaching royalty rights to the end product. Recently some institutions have become more directly involved in the development and testing stages by forming joint stock companies for the purpose of taking equity stakes in the new business.

9.18   It is now a year since the Muir Wood Report (ACARD/ABRC, *Improving research links between higher education and industry*, HMSO, 1983) proposed the establishment of an industrial "seedcorn" fund as an incentive to universities to seek further links with industry and commerce. We strongly support this. **We recommend that the Government should provide additional funds for the establishment of an industrial "seedcorn" fund.**

9.19   Many of our respondents believed that it was possible for universities to increase their income from services rendered to clients in the private and public sectors both here and overseas. There are encouraging signs to support this belief. Research income from industry and commerce and from Government bodies other than Research Councils both increased by an estimated 20 per cent between 1979-80 and 1982-83. Many universities have established consultancy companies or appointed industrial liaison officers to foster collaboration. There are already a number of science parks, and it has been suggested that these can be a source of income for universities. We do not believe that they can, at least under present Treasury rules. A science park is of considerable benefit to a university because of the improved contacts with industry and the general intellectual stimulus it generates. It should not be seen as a milch cow.

9.20   We must also sound three notes of caution. The first is that, while income from services rendered increases the level of university activity, it is only the excess of income over the associated expenditure that is available to contribute to the funding of basic teaching and research. Even when there is an excess it will be small. It does not remove the need for basic teaching and research to be publicly funded.

9.21   Second, the search by universities for additional income for services rendered incurs substantial administrative costs and makes considerable demands on the time of senior academic staff. There must be a point at which the benefit of securing extra income is outweighed by the loss to non-commercial teaching and research.

9.22   Third, if universities place excessive reliance on income from services rendered they are in danger of distorting academic balance by emphasising short-term applied work in the sciences at the expense of basic research. There are some subject areas even in the sciences for which there is no obvious commercial market.

Separate funding of selected institutions

9.23   From time to time suggestions are made for more radical schemes for financing a small number of universities with the long-term objective of reducing their dependence on UGC funds. One scheme which received attention in 1983 involved paying a university a single budget containing all the public funds it and its students would receive, except possibly Research Council grants. The university would then decide its own student number targets, fix its own fees and manage its own capital assets. We would be prepared to advise on any such scheme if asked to do so. Nevertheless we doubt whether this concept, as a first stage towards complete independence from public support, could be of wide application to institutions with the range of functions which universities perform.

9.24   Finally, although as we said in para 9.11 home student fees cannot be regarded as payments for services rendered, there may be scope for generating some additional fee income. The present arrangements for the public funding of students on one year taught postgraduate courses are limited in their scope and aims. A relatively small amount of public money is directed selectively by the Research Councils towards the support of the best courses and the ablest students, so securing a base of academic excellence. In our view it is in the national interest that these general arrangements should continue. **We see advantages, however, in an increase in the number of postgraduate students who are not financed from public funds.** Some taught courses provide advanced and post-experience education of direct and immediate value to industry and commerce. The contribution which students from such courses can make is recognised in the high financial rewards available to them. Many of the students already pay their own fees and maintenance costs. We believe that the public interest would be well served if more students were encouraged to follow their example. The wider availability of commercial loan schemes to assist students with these costs would be a valuable addition to the present public support arrangements.

Section 10

The organisation of individual universities

Size of universities and departments

10.1 Institutions vary in size from 800 students at Lampeter to 12,000 at Manchester (excluding UMIST). The University of London with its many colleges and schools has some 49,000 internal students. We believe in a considerable diversity within the university system, and it would be absurd to suggest that there is an optimum size or shape for a university. But to assume that the present mixture is right would be to place undue reliance on serendipity.

10.2 There are subjects, such as art and design, which by historical accident lie almost entirely in the public sector. There are also subjects which do not yet contain a sufficient agreed body of knowledge to justify teaching, and there are subjects in which student demand is so small that only the presence of an outstanding scholar justifies their retention. But broadly speaking, the university system should maintain a presence in every branch of knowledge and that presence should be of international standard. This is true alike in the humanities and in the science — both in potentially wealth-creating subjects and in those whose justification is primarily cultural.

10.3 But what is valid for the system as a whole need not be valid for any of its individual components. It used to be accepted that each university, or at any rate each major university, should cover all important branches of knowledge. But knowledge has vastly increased in the last thirty years, both by the appearance of new subjects and by advances in traditional ones. At the same time individual academics have tended to specialise more than they used to do, both in their research and in their teaching. Comprehensive coverage for research has become impossible for any university, probably even for London. Comprehensive coverage for teaching has in many cases led universities to spread their resources too thinly.

10.4 In any subject the number of places that should be provided in the university system must be limited by the number of well-qualified candidates. In subjects in which demand is modest there can only be a limited number of departments if they are not to fall below an economic size. The dispersion of resources among small departments acts against the creation of departments of international standing. A small department in a large subject need not be weak, provided it is selective in its interests; but we are concerned at the number of small departments that are also weak departments. **We believe that in a good many subjects there will have to be fewer departments than there are now.**

Rationalisation

10.5 How the rationalisation of small departments is to be achieved will be one of the major problems of the next few years. We have asked each of our subject sub-committees to make a detailed study of the issues involved in its field. We expect to give more advice to universities than in the past but we hope that, having done so, we shall be able to leave much of the initiative to them and that we shall only need to play an enabling role. **In allocating funds we shall discriminate in favour of universities which tackle the problem of small departments.** Rationalisation will give better value for money in the long run but we recognise that temporary extra expenditure may be needed to bring it about.

10.6 Every university will have to accept that there is a choice to be made between covering many subjects patchily and covering fewer subjects adequately. If a university feels it must retain all those subjects which it has supported in the past, then it will have no room to take on the new subjects which are likely to be growth-points of the future. It must create, both in student numbers and in finance, scope to develop new subjects and new areas within subjects. This can be done only at the expense of areas whose relative importance is decreasing.

10.7 Institutions already share a significant amount of teaching, largely in subjects that attract small numbers of students. We welcome the fact that this happens across the binary line as well as within the university sector and we wish to encourage it. However, although shared teaching ameliorates the disadvantages of too many small departments, it does not altogether remedy them — for even if a lecturer comes from another institution to give a course of lectures, he will not be regularly available for consultation in the way that he would be in his home university.

10.8   The most radical way of increasing the size of departments and diminishing their number is by the merger of institutions. Mergers are at the moment a fashionable idea. Because of this we need to sound a note of warning. There are two kinds of claim that can be made for any particular merger: that it promotes efficiency, or that it creates a strong institution out of two or more weaker ones. A formal merger in which as little as possible is changed will not achieve either of these: to achieve them, merger will have to be combined with reorganisation. It takes surprisingly long for the full effects of a merger to be achieved: Imperial College was created by a merger of three institutions before the First World War, but it still retains traces of the individual components. Whatever the eventual gains of mergers there is temporary disruption and it takes considerable time before economies are realised.

The government and management of universities

10.9   The two principal bodies in a typical university are the Council (Court in Scotland) and the Senate. The Council has a responsibility for everything that affects the finances of the university, and the Senate has a responsibility for everything that affects its academic work. Most important issues concern both bodies. When universities were expanding, the major decisions were where growth should take place: that was clearly a matter for the Senate within the financial guidelines laid down by the Council. The worsening climate of the last ten years has already placed much more responsibility on the Council. For the rest of this century at least, financial limitations will be a severe constraint on universities, and they will have to make hard choices. It will be tempting to back too many options because temporary economies can always be made by postponing necessary expenditure, and better times may be just around the corner. It is not usually for the Council to make the choices, but part of its responsibility is to ensure that hard decisions are faced and choices are made.

10.10   In a typical university leadership must come primarily from the Vice-Chancellor. It falls to him more than to anyone else to overcome institutional inertia. He must motivate staff to recognise the need for long-term change and to participate in planning it and carrying it out. He must manage his university both for survival and for excellence. He must see that it plans and controls its use of resources so that it is not blown off course by short-term financial pressures. He must ensure that it can respond to new opportunities while preserving and expanding its existing areas of excellence.

10.11   In the universities tradition and inertia often work against change. In particular, in the Senate the practitioners of existing subjects are present to make their case, while the practitioners of the potential new subjects are not. Universities need to acquire what they now lack: a deliberate bias towards change.

10.12   This criticism is not the only one that can be made of the machinery of government of universities. Much of the activity of academics consists of re-examining received notions; and it is an axiom that, however decisive an argument may appear to be, one must not rule out the possibility that new and unforeseeable considerations may undermine it. In research, which is a perfectionist activity, this is essential. Everyday administration should not be like that, but typically decisions in a university are put forward by a subordinate committee and then reconsidered by a hierarchy of further committees piled on top of it. This may improve the quality of the decisions, but at the price of a great deal of delay and a great diversion of the time and energy of academics from their prime functions of teaching and research. In our judgement the cost often outweighs the gain. The position has become more serious in the last few years, because contraction is inevitably more controversial than expansion. We have been struck by the number of complaints we have heard from academics that they have been distracted from teaching and research by the increasing number of committees on which they have to serve.

10.13   Some universities have a more elaborate and unwieldy structure of government than others. **We believe that every university should examine its machinery of government, to ensure that its decision-making processes are effective.**

Section 11

The organisation of Higher Education: National level

Coordination and cooperation

11.1 The Government's higher education policy must be consistent with its general social and economic policies, and major strategic decisions on higher education must fall to Ministers. There are some institutions with which Government Departments deal directly but for the most part the development and coordination of higher education in accordance with Ministers' general strategy are left to various advisory bodies. Those bodies are: the UGC for universities in the United Kingdom; the National Advisory Body for Local Authority Higher Education (NAB) for polytechnics and other local authority colleges in England and now for voluntary colleges; and the Wales Advisory Body (WAB) for local authority colleges in Wales. In Scotland a Scottish Tertiary Education Advisory Council (STEAC) has just been established, though with much less responsibility than the other three bodies.

11.2 The institutions with which these bodies are concerned differ in their origins and character and in many other ways. It is not surprising therefore that the bodies themselves differ in composition, functions and working methods. The question is whether they can carry out their own tasks adequately and cooperate effectively with one another.

11.3 The great majority of our respondents favoured the continuation, though perhaps with some modification, of the existing bodies. Only a few advocated radical change—for example, a unitary system of post-school education under some form of local or regional control. There was little support for such possibilities as combining the UGC with NAB and WAB, or for having a separate UGC for Scotland, or for establishing an overarching body to stand between Ministers and the UGC and the other bodies.

11.4 We think the majority is right. In paras 11.14-20 we argue for the continuation of our own role but suggest ways in which our operations should be improved. NAB and WAB are still new and STEAC has only just been constituted. This is not the time for further radical change. But it is essential that all four bodies cooperate closely and effectively. An overarching body will then be unnecessary.

11.5 Endorsement of existing administrative arrangements implies endorsement of the policy of successive Governments to develop two complementary sectors of higher education, of equal standing but of different characters and serving different purposes. We do indeed support in broad principle the continuence of the binary system. We believe that the condition for the inclusion of institutions on our grant list should be that they should have a substantial commitment to both teaching and research and should be funded accordingly. However it does not follow that, because an institution has a certain role now and is funded through a particular channel, there is no possibility of a change in the future. Indeed we have referred in para 8.16-17 to the possibility that, if the funds available to us were insufficient to support all institutions on our grant list, we might have to recommend to the Secretary of State that one or more of them should be removed from it.

11.6 The UGC and NAB advise the same Secretary of State. We are confident that the relations which we have already established with NAB, and which we intend to develop, will ensure that the views which either body offers him will take due account of the views of the other. We are confident too that consistency can be preserved between our advice, planning and decision-making for the university sector and NAB's advice, planning and decision-making for the public sector in England. The Welsh education system is essentially the same as the English one except for the important role played by the Welsh language. WAB takes part in our discussions with NAB, and has other direct dealings with NAB. There is a need, though, for consultation at the regional as well as the national level. **As a step towards this, we believe that the universities in England and Wales should develop their links with the higher education committees of the Regional Advisory Councils.**

11.7 In Scotland secondary education has for long been more broadly based than in the rest of the United Kingdom. Two consequences are that honours degree courses are a year longer than elsewhere and that Scottish school-leavers can have difficulty in gaining entry to higher education institutions elsewhere. Scotland therefore needs special consideration in the planning of higher education. It is frequently said that the UGC has not taken enough account of the special features of Scotland. Some critics have even raised the possibility of a separate Scottish UGC. We believe that this would be disadvantageous to the Scottish universities, because it would tend to separate them from the rest of the university system in the United Kingdom. But we recognise the need for better coordination of higher education in Scotland. STEAC's first task is "to consider and report on the future strategy for higher education in Scotland, including the arrangements for providing institutions with financial support, and the general principles which should govern relationships between universities and other institutions". We shall be elaborating our views on these matters to STEAC. However we note that it is not a permanent body, and it does not have powers to recommend the grants for the central institutions and colleges of education. We hope that STEAC's review will result in stable arrangements under which close cooperation in the planning of higher education in Scotland will be possible.

11.8   In Northern Ireland universities and colleges alike are directly funded by the Department of Education for Northern Ireland (DENI). The University of Ulster, which is being formed through the merger of the Ulster Polytechnic and the New University of Ulster, will be expected to perform the functions both of a university and of a polytechnic. Its grant, and that of Queen's University, Belfast, will be determined by DENI on the advice of the UGC. This has broadened our responsibilities in several ways. We have therefore set up for a period a Northern Ireland Working Party, with a strong public sector element, to help us to extend our knowledge of the Province.

11.9   We have referred to our relations with the Research Councils and the ABRC in Section 5. We also value our contacts with the AUT, the NUS and the non-academic staff unions. However, the pre-eminent role at national level in conveying the universities' views to the Committee must fall to the CVCP. Contacts between the Chairman and officers of the CVCP and the UGC have always been close and at intervals there have been meetings of small groups of members. Last winter, as part of the preliminaries to the preparation of this advice, there was a two day meeting between the whole Committee and the General Purposes Committee of the CVCP. We hope to hold similar joint meetings at intervals. More generally, we intend wherever possible to make use of the advice and experience of the CVCP.

The UGC's own role and functions

11.10   Our terms of reference give us four tasks:

(i) to enquire into the financial needs of university education in the United Kingdom;

(ii) to advise the Government as to the application of any grants made by Parliament towards meeting them;

(iii) to collect, examine and make available information relating to university education throughout the United Kingdom;

(iv) to assist, in consultation with the universities and other bodies concerned, the preparation and execution of such plans for development of the universities as may from time to time be required in order to ensure that they are fully adequate to national needs.

11.11   The first and fourth tasks go together. We welcome the fact that the Secretary of State has reasserted them by asking for our views on future strategy, after a period in which we have been primarily concerned with cutting back. Now that development is no longer a synonym for growth, we recognise that the fourth task is considerably more intricate than in the past.

11.12   The third of our tasks is primarily a matter of administrative action. There is always a risk that statistics may continue to be collected long after the original requirement has passed. The process must therefore be reviewed periodically. Such a review has been carried out in the last few years. One important by-product is that university statistics now become available for use much earlier than before.

11.13   The second of our tasks has dominated the work of the Committee for at least ten years and has become increasingly difficult as funds have been reduced. Our main job has been to make the best use of such resources as the Government has provided. In 1981 the Committee made the dispositions which in the circumstances it judged were the best possible for the system generally and for the country, while recognising that this meant the sacrifice of much that was undoubtedly good. Its decisions on those institutions which were hit hardest have been strongly criticised. Indeed it has been said that the Committee lost much of its credibility in 1981.

11.14 Some respondents have asserted that the Committee is not properly constituted to discharge its functions and should be replaced by a representative body with members drawn from interest groups. It has also been argued that we have two kinds of function which call for two different kinds of body — one executive and the other advisory. We consider that a representative body would be ill-constituted to handle the executive function, which must increasingly involve selectivity; and it would also be unsuitable for the advisory function, for even if it did not take on the role of a pressure group for universities it would be thought to have done so and its advice would be correspondingly discounted by Government. In any case the two functions require so nearly the same knowledge and are so closely connected that it would be an administrative extravagance to set up separate bodies to carry them out. **We recommend that the role of the Committee should remain largely unchanged** but, as we indicate below there are ways in which our operations can be improved.

11.15 We intend to be more open about our decisions and advice than in the past. In particular we aim to give a rather more detailed explanation of the grants to individual institutions. This may have some disadvantages for universities, for it is bound to affect the internal debate on how the grant should be divided up. We shall be consulting the CVCP on this.

11.16 The Chairman of the UGC has always had ready access to Ministers. This has been of great value to the Committee and to the universities. **We hope that it will also be possible for the whole Committee or for groups of members to meet Ministers more frequently than in the past.**

11.17 We need to be constantly in touch with the universities, to help us both to advise Government on their needs and to judge how they are likely to respond to any initiatives which we are considering. We already have many contacts, formal and informal, with individual universities and we hope to develop them. We intend to consider the frequency and the organisation of visits by the Committee and the sub-committees in order to ensure that they are as useful as possible. **The recently introduced practice of seconding university administrators to our secretariat has already proved its value. We hope that this practice will continue and if possible grow.**

11.18 What the Committee can do is limited by the demands which it can make on its members and by the size of its staff and budget. Members are appointed on the understanding that they will give an average of one-fifth of their time to the job. In fact they now need to give much more than this, particularly those members who are chairmen of the various sub-committees. The load on members of the sub-committees has also increased.

11.19 The combined staff of the UGC and of NAB is less than the central staff of even the smallest Research Council. We accept that this is not comparing like with like, but it seems to imply that in the eyes of those who control our staffing the UGC and NAB combined are expected to know less, and do less, than even the smallest Research Council. What justifies the staffing levels of the Research Councils is that they have to operate an allocation system which is both open and discriminatory. Increasingly we shall have to do the same, and this will involve restoring part of the substantial cut which has been made in our staffing since 1979. That cut has already caused a deterioration in the level of service which we can provide to universities; and they have made it clear to us that they believe we are now understaffed.

11.20 Finally we must remark on the low level of technology permitted in the UGC office. Given that we have to administer such large sums of public money, it is essential that the office is properly provided for. The fact that we have been designated as a cost centre has given us only very limited freedom to introduce modern equipment. We accept that the UGC may be no worse off than many Government offices. Nevertheless, we would severely criticise any university whose central offices were as ill-provided as ours.

Conclusion 11.21   The Committee's aim in July 1981 was to minimise the damage to the system caused by the cuts imposed by Government. But those cuts were so severe that great harm has still been done. Academic planning has been disrupted, morale has been impaired, thousands of young people have been denied a university education, confidence in Government has been shaken and will be difficult to restore. Expenditure has been reduced as Government required, but the university system left by the cuts is not ideal for meeting the nation's future needs. To secure full effectiveness and flexibility, further restructuring is necessary. New courses must be established, research must be strengthened, unsuitable and redundant buildings must be sold or demolished, full advantage must be taken of advances in technology to increase the effectiveness of teaching, staffing problems must be overcome, organisation must be improved. It is for these purposes, not to maintain the present position, still less to restore the past, that in this advice we have pressed for adequate resources and an adequate planning horizon. Without them the prospect is of further disruption and decline.

11.22   The UGC stands between Government and the universities as it has done for 65 years. Recent difficulties have led to its being criticised more than before; but they have also shown that an intermediary body is still essential. We are not the servants either of Government or of the universities. As one half of our task we shall continue to assert to Government the needs of the universities for resources which will enable them to provide teaching and research of the highest quality as they must always aim to do. As the other half of our task we shall guide and encourage universities towards the changes which we are convinced they must make, and are willing to make, in order to serve the national interest into the 1990s and beyond.

Section 12
Summary of recommendations

Student numbers:

(i) Provision for home initial entrants over the three years 1985–86 to 1987–88 should move progressively closer to the level of demand shown in the DES 1984 Variant X, ie to about 170,000, and should be held at that level until the end of the decade.

(ii) Full-time home postgraduates in the universities should be enabled to rise from about 31,000 in 1983–84 to about 36,000 by the end of the decade; of these 16,000 should be research students and 20,000 on taught courses.

(iii) Taking (i) and (ii) together and allowing for students from abroad, including those from the European Community, numbers in higher education should rise to about 600,000 full-time and sandwich students in Great Britain.

(iv) Neither the Variant X nor the Variant Y projection is reliable for the longer term. In order to provide a sounder basis for planning for the 1990s the projections should be reconsidered and recalculated in three or four years' time. On that occasion separate projections based on the same principles should be made for Scotland.

(v) Efforts should be made meanwhile to improve the coverage and quality of the data used for the projections. (para 2.12)

The Education Departments and the Research Councils should seek funds to reverse the decline in the number of postgraduate research studentships. (para 5.24)

There should be a minimum annual recruitment of 3.5 per cent of the total number of academic staff. This would imply at least 900 new appointments a year. (para 7.5)

The Government should make additional funds available to enable the Committee to reimburse universities with 50 per cent of the cost of compensation under the Premature Retirement Compensation Scheme. (para 7.7)

The present machinery for the negotiation of non-clinical academic salaries should be reviewed. (para 7.29)

The Government should at a minimum provide truly level funding of recurrent grant at least until the end of the decade, which is the period for which we have made recommendations on student numbers. (para 8.6)

The Government should introduce a longer planning horizon for recurrent grant. (para 8.21)

The equipment grant should immediately be increased to the level indicated by the equipment grant model (that is, by at least 25 per cent) and should not again fall below it. (para 8.33)

The capital grant should be held at its current value in real terms for the next two years, but should then be sympathetically reviewed. (para 8.37)

The retention limit of £100,000 on the proceeds of sale of property should be doubled. In circumstances where the Committee's prior approval is required universities should be allowed to retain the entire proceeds, whatever the amount. (para 8.39)

The Committee's delegated authority should be extended so that it is able to cover all aspects of universities' capital proposals. (para 8.40)

The Government should make an explicit statement revoking the principle of deficiency funding so as to encourage universities and potential donors. (para 9.9)

The Government should consider changes in the tax laws which would help universities to raise more income. (para 9.10)

It should be drawn to the attention of Government Departments that they should meet the full cost of the research which they commission in universities. (para 9.16)

The Government should provide additional funds for the establishment of an industrial "seedcorn" fund. (para 9.18)

The role of the Committee should remain largely unchanged. (para 11.14)

Annex A

Circular Letter 16/83

To all Vice-Chancellors and Principals

1 November 1983

Dear Vice-Chancellor/Principal,

Development of a strategy for Higher Education into the 1990s

INTRODUCTION
You will probably have seen already the recent exchange of correspondence between the Secretary of State for Education and Science and my predecessor: however, for ease of reference, I attach a copy at Annex A*. The Secretary of State asks for a debate on the issues that face higher education over the next ten years; and he asks that this debate should be conducted in as open and wide-ranging a manner as possible. This letter is the Committee's first step towards encouraging such a debate.

2 The Committee will be giving the Secretary of State its advice not later than October 1984 and wishes to take full account of the contributions of universities and other interested parties. We could simply have invited comments on the Secretary of State's letter; but we believe it will be more helpful if we try to list the questions which we consider the Committee should cover in its advice and which participants in the debate should think about, whether or not they feel it reasonable for them to answer them at this stage.

3 With two exceptions, we do not ask your university *as such* to answer these questions, because there is likely to be a great diversity of views within each university and nothing will be gained by disguising this fact. The two exceptions are Questions 1 and 2, which are addressed to institutions and not to groups within them. We would be grateful to receive replies to these two questions by 31 March 1984.

4 It is, of course, open to your university, if it wishes, to comment on any of the remaining questions: indeed we hope that it would at least be able to answer Questions 8 and 13. We would also ask you to encourage general debate on these issues within your university and we would welcome comments from groups and individuals, whether in the form of answers to particular questions or otherwise. Some of the questions — 4, for example — are ones on which we would particularly value the answers of those officers who have been concerned with the relevant problems. In particular, we hope that you yourself will be able to comment on some of the issues as an individual. On Questions 28 and 29, for example, the experience of Vice-Chancellors must give their views especial authority. Again we would ask for replies by 31 March 1984 but where it is possible we would appreciate earlier replies to spread the load.

5 The Secretary of State has asked the National Advisory Body for Local Authority Higher Education (NAB) to encourage the same kind of debate in respect of the public sector institutions for which it is responsible. NAB's first step has been to produce a consultation paper "Towards a Strategy for Local Authority Higher Education in the Late 1980s and Beyond", and a copy of this is attached at Annex B†. It is clear that there will have to be an eventual reconciliation between the replies of NAB and UGC to the Secretary of State.

6 Parts of this letter refer primarily to the situation in England and Wales. We would ask readers concerned with the different systems in Scotland and Northern Ireland to make the appropriate adjustments.

RESOURCES AND STUDENT NUMBERS
7 We see no possibility of the resource per student (ie home fees plus recurrent grant) being increased in real terms, except, we would hope, to take account of a shift in the balance of students from cheaper to more expensive subjects. Indeed the Secretary of State suggests that we should consider the possibility of a cut in the resource per student of up to 2 per cent in real terms in each of the next five years and of up to 1 per cent in each of the following five years. At the same time he hopes that universities will move towards raising a greater proportion of their income from private sources, thus reducing their dependence on public funds.

8 The DES has revised its earlier calculations of the demand for higher education and has also produced forecasts of total numbers in higher education which are based on a high and a low projection of the proportion of qualified demand being met. These projections are given in Annex C*.

9 On the DES's high demand projection, numbers remain at or above the 1983-84 level until 1988-89. Between then and 1996-97 they drop by almost 20 per cent, after which there is a small recovery until the end of the century. On the low demand projection, numbers do not fall below the 1983-84 projected level until 1987-88, after which they drop by 5 per cent by 1989-90 and a further 20 per cent between 1989-90 and 1996-97, with a small recovery during the rest of the century. It must be emphasised that these projections assume that the present distribution of lengths of courses will remain unchanged; and any major changes in the pattern of higher education (for example, those discussed in paras 29 and 30) are likely to affect the figures for total numbers of students.

10 It would be unrealistic to expect the drop in the number of qualified school-leavers to be compensated by an increase in the average length of course. However there is the possibility of a growth in some of the various forms of continuing education. The Committee has a working party on this topic, which sent you a substantial questionnaire some months ago and which is expected to report early next year. In this letter, therefore, we are not asking the range of questions on continuing education which would otherwise have been appropriate, but it does come up in Question 17. I would only say that, provided a number of problems can be solved (for example, in the area of the student support), there is the potential for substantial development of continuing education, though it cannot be assumed that this will make good the loss of initial students resulting from the demographic trends.

11 It will be clear from para 9 that the demand projections for the next five years and for the five that follow pose quite different problems. For the next five years the obvious questions are the following:

Q.1 **On the assumption of (a) constant numbers of home and EC students and (b) constant resource per student in real terms from 1983–84 to 1989–90 inclusive, what changes will your institution want to make and how do you plan to achieve them?**

Q.2 **How would the answer to the previous question be affected if student numbers in this period were to remain constant but the resource per student in real terms were to drop at a steady rate of:**

(a) **1 per cent per annum?**

(b) **2 per cent per annum?**

12 In a number of subjects, notably medicine, dentistry, veterinary science and education, the number of students depends on the Government's policies on manpower requirements. This external factor creates obvious constraints and pressures on resources but for the purpose of answering Questions 1 and 2 you should assume that the current policies continue at least until 1989-90.

13 For the five years that follow, (ie from 1990-91 to 1994-95), and indeed to the turn of the century, it is difficult to consider the university system in isolation, because we do not know how any reduction in higher education

---
*Annex A is not reproduced here but is published in the UGC's *Annual Survey 1982-83*, Cmnd 9234, as Appendices E and F.
†Annex B is not reproduced here.

*Annex C is not reproduced here but was based on DES Report on Education Number 99 (1983).

numbers resulting from the drop in the number of qualified school-leavers will be distributed between the universities and the public sector. But any shift of balance will only diminish the problems of one side by exacerbating those of the other. Some further reduction in the resource per student in real terms must be accepted as a possibility — the Secretary of State has suggested that we should consider a figure of 5 per cent over the years 1990-91 to 1994-95 — but its effect can only be small in comparison with the effect of falling numbers.

> **Q.3** On the assumption of constant resource per student in real terms from 1990-91 to the end of the century, how should the higher education system as a whole cope with student numbers dropping by 15-20 per cent between 1989-90 and 1994-95 and remaining constant thereafter? What scope is there for reorganisation? Do you see mergers or other forms of association between universities and public sector institutions as desirable and practicable? What scope is there for greater collaboration? Should a significant number of institutions be closed during the five years 1990-91 to 1994-95? If so, what criteria and what machinery should be used to decide which institutions to close?

CAPITAL

14 The Secretary of State did not refer in his letter to the provision of funds for capital building but it is likely that resources will be extremely limited.

> **Q.4** How might any necessary reorganisation be financed from recurrent grant and proceeds of sale? Are the conditions which apply at present to the use of proceeds of sale or any other rules relating to the use for capital purposes of resources from public funds unduly restrictive? If so, what changes would be helpful?

BALANCE OF SUBJECTS

15 The Secretary of State is anxious to see a shift towards technological, scientific and engineering courses and towards other vocationally relevant forms of study, and has asked how, and how fast, this can be achieved. Universities can of course shift the balance of their admissions, so far as their accommodation permits; but this could merely mean admitting more marginal candidates in the sciences and fewer in the arts. The Secretary of State also wishes to see a shift of balance among the first-class candidates. This would require changes in the schools or the provision of conversion courses.

> **Q.5** Does your experience suggest that there would be a demand for conversion courses? If so, how and in what kind of institution might it be appropriate to provide them? Can you see any other way of meeting the Secretary of State's wishes?

16 Even without deliberate pressure, changes in student choice are likely to change the balance of student numbers. This ought to be reflected in a similar change in the balance of staff numbers which will not be easy in a period in which there will be very little flexibility; indeed it can only exacerbate the difficulties noted in the next few paragraphs.

> **Q.6** Which subjects do you expect to become more popular, and which less popular, over the next decade?
>
> **Q.7** Are there other reasons why you would wish to favour some subjects at the expense of others?

RESEARCH

17 In the natural sciences (in the widest sense) there is a reasonably clear distinction between scholarship and research. Scholarship means keeping abreast of the current state of one's own subject, and may include writing books and papers which expound and systematise what is known: research means advancing what is known. It is harder to draw this distinction in the social sciences, and harder still in the arts. It is axiomatic that scholarship is part of the duty of every teacher in higher education (regardless of sector) and that higher education institutions must make adequate provision for scholarship — which includes provision for libraries and for travel. But research in some subjects requires facilities additional to those needed for scholarship; and in some subjects these facilities are expensive. In all subjects the largest component of university research is the thinking time of staff, which it is extremely difficult to quantify.

18 It is widely believed that the cuts of the last few years have fallen more heavily on research (and in particular on scientific research) than on teaching. This appears not to be what the Government would have wished, as is shown by, for example, the degree of protection that has been given to the Science Budget.

> **Q.8** Do you think that this has happened in your institution? Have you any quantitative evidence that bears on this question? If it has happened in your institution, are you taking, or do you intend to take, any counter-measures?
>
> **Q.9** Do you think that the dual support system can survive and would you wish it to do so?
>
> **Q.10** Would you favour earmarking, or indicating, the research component of the UGC grant? If so, what items of expenditure would be covered by this earmarking or indicating?
>
> **Q.11** The Secretary of State has suggested that greater selectivity of research funding may be needed, both within institutions and between institutions. What are your views on this?
>
> **Q.12** What priorities, if any, would you suggest for special research investment (beyond those already identified, such as micro-electronics, information techonolgy and biotechnology)?

DEPENDENCE ON PUBLIC FUNDS

19 As I said in para 7, the Secretary of State believes that universities ought to reduce their dependence on public funds — which include student fees reimbursed by local education authorities. He has already held discussions about ways in which this might be achieved with a number of Vice-Chancellors, at which my predecessor was present. These discussions have not yet led to a clear or agreed solution, but it is apparent that any solution involves giving individual universities greater freedom from the control of the DES and the UGC; and this is a policy to which the Secretary of State is attracted for other reasons also.

> **Q.13** Are there respects in which you would wish your university to have greater freedom from the control of DES and UGC? What do you see as the financial advantages of this? And the non-financial advantages? What scope do you see for raising additional income, whether tied to specific purposes or not? Could the prospects be improved by a change in the tax laws? If so, what?

THE NATURE OF UNIVERSITIES

20 The binary line and, more generally, the differences between universities and major public sector institutions are currently a topic for debate. There are three headings under which these differences can be considered — the interface with Government to which I revert in paras 31 and 32, the constitutional differences, one of which is touched on in para 21, and the differences of function.

> **Q.14** Is there an essential difference in function between universities and other institutions of higher education, or should they be regarded as a continuous spectrum of institutions?
>
> **Q.15** If there is an essential difference in their teaching function, what is it, and how, in measurable terms, can one distinguish between those school-leavers who would benefit most from university-type education and those who would benefit most from other types of higher education?
>
> **Q.16** Should there be more variety among universities in respect, for example, of disciplinary specialisation, type of student

(mature, overseas etc), teaching style and involvement in research?

Q.17 Do you have views on a desirable balance in the university system, between provision for:

(i) Undergraduates, taught postgraduates and research postgraduates?

(ii) initial and post-experience provision?

(iii) full-time, sandwich and part-time provision?

In what ways does your view of the desirable balance for your own institution differ from your view of the desirable balance for the system as a whole?

VALIDATION

21 Almost all public sector courses are validated by external bodies — mainly by CNAA and BTEC. Some university courses are accredited in varying degrees by professional bodies — in law, medicine or engineering, for example — and all university courses have external examiners who play a certain moderating role.

Q.18 What is your experience of the process of accreditation by professional bodies in those subjects in which they operate? What are your views on any other possible system of accreditation or validation of university courses?

TENURE AND PREMATURE RETIREMENT

22 Universities largely coped with the 1981 cuts by means of early retirements. This has left a very unbalanced age distribution of academic staff: detailed figures, broken down by subject, are given in Annex D*. The Annex also shows how the overall age distribution will vary up to the end of the century, on the assumption that all posts falling vacant will be filled. This is essentially the assumption of constant level of support per student and constant student numbers. For comments on these assumptions see paras 7 and 9. Even on these assumptions the rate of new appointments in most subjects during the next decade will be between 1 per cent and 1½ per cent per annum in the system as a whole; and in many universities it will be well below that. For comparison, in its proposal last year for "new blood" posts the ABRC argued, and the DES accepted, that a replacement rate of 1¼ per cent was the least that could keep a subject in good health. (The argument was concerned with research rather than teaching, and it was put forward only for the sciences; but this estimate remains the only one available.)

23 For the next five years, therefore, the replacement rate will be slightly below the acceptable minimum even on the most favourable hypothesis (ie that the level of support per student will be constant in real terms) and a *nil* replacement rate is not unlikely. The continuation of the new blood scheme must be a possibility, even though it could involve the Government giving new money with one hand while taking away existing money with the other. But if this happened it would almost certainly be operated in a highly selective way.

Q.19 Would you favour the continuation of the new blood scheme? What do you see as its disadvantages and to what extent can they be overcome?

Q.20 What other realistic ways do you see of overcoming the problems of the next five years outlined in paras 22–23?

24 For the five years 1990-91 to 1994-95, the position is far more serious. If student numbers fall as projected and the balance between the university and the public sector is maintained, the size of the university sector will drop by 15–20 per cent. At most, half of the necessary reduction in staff can be obtained from normal retirements; and the Secretary of State has made it clear that the Government is not prepared to find extra money to pay for premature retirements after the end of the current academic year.

Q.21 Would you favour reducing the retiring age to 60, with the possibility of extending some academic staff beyond 60 on a non-tenured basis? (It is accepted that this would require legislation.)

25 One of the main reasons why contraction presents far greater difficulties for unversities than for most other enterprises is the existence of tenure, so that appointments cannot be terminated before normal retirement age other than for "good cause". In some universities the tenure provision is strong, in others it is weak, and in yet others the combined effect of statutes and conditions of appointment is so obscure that it could only be determined in the courts.

Q.23 Should the tenure provisions be the same in all universities? If so, what should they be? If not, would there be any long-term consequences?

THE LEVERHULME PROPOSALS

26 The most recent programme of study of higher education is the series of conferences and reports organised by the Society for Research into Higher Education and financed by the Leverhulme Trust. Some of the proposals in the final volume "Excellence in Diversity" have already been covered in this letter, but there are two important ones which have not. These are:

(a) the reduction of specialisation both in the sixth form and in the earlier parts of higher education; and

(b) the reorganisation of higher education into a sequence of two year modules.

27 Neither of these changes could come about quickly, if only because of the preparatory work that would be involved. Thus if they are to be set in a particular context, that context should be the declining number of 18 year olds between 1989-90 and 1994-95, or the constant but lower numbers in the following five years.

28 One of the major acknowledged disadvantages of the present degree of specialisation in the sixth form is that decisions taken by school-children at the age of 15 or 16 often restrict their choice of degree courses two or three years later. The amount of specialisation in the sixth form is, of course, greatly influenced by the demands of universities. There is a considerable body of opinion among school heads in favour of a broader sixth form curriculum, but they say that they cannot themselves implement such a policy because it would put their pupils at a disadvantage in the competition for university places.

Q.24 Would you favour the universal replacement of the present system of A-levels by a broader sixth form education and, if so, on what pattern? What would this imply for the quality and skills of your graduates?

Q.25 Alternatively, would you favour making a broader sixth form education available to those who preferred it? If so, would you be willing to see your university's admission criteria altered so that students with a broader sixth form education were not at a disadvantage in applying for admission to your university?

29 An initial two year non-vocational module within higher education already exists, in the form of the Diploma of Higher Education; but it has not gained much support because it is generally seen as inferior to a three-year degree. (The two-year course at Buckingham is not wholly relevant, because the academic year there is substantially longer.) Moreover there would be serious problems in transfers between a university based on two-year modules and a university with the present structure of courses, whereas now students have no problems in taking a first degree in one university and then going on to postgraduate work in another. So if a change to a sequence of two-year modules is to happen at all, it needs to happen simultaneously in as many universities as possible.

Q.26 Would you favour such a change?

30 There have also been suggestions (though not in the Leverhulme report) that the structure of university courses in England and Wales should

*Annex D is not reproduced here.

be modified somewhat along the lines of the present structure in Scotland, where there is choice between a general and an honours degree. In such a scheme there would be choice between a two year general degree and a three year honours degree: whether the choice would be made at entry or after one year at university is an open question.

- Q.27 **Would you favour such a change, or indeed, any other change in degree format (including a longer academic year)?**

THE ROLE OF THE UGC

31 The role of the UGC has changed very considerably since it was set up in 1919, and it may change further in the next few years.

- Q.28 **Have you any comments on the nature and role of the UGC, or on the way in which it should carry out that role?**

32 There have been suggestions that a single body should be set up to take over some or all of the work of the UGC and, for example, NAB and the Wales Advisory Body, either replacing them or standing between them and Government.

- Q.29 **Do you favour such a proposal, and if so in what form? More generally, do you see centralised coordination of both sectors as either desirable or feasible?**

Yours sincerely

Peter Swinnerton-Dyer

Annex B

Respondents to Circular Letter 16/83

On receipt each reply was placed in one of five categories, A to E, and allotted a serial number in that category. A few replies have since been reallocated to a different category but have retained their original serial numbers. In several cases similar but not necessarily identical replies from given respondents were received and these letters have been cross-referenced in this index. With these cases counted once only, replies were received from a total of 658 respondents:

- 55 from institutions on the UGC's grant list and the Northern Ireland universities (category A)
- 11 from vice-chancellors and principals of institutions on the UGC's grant list (category B)
- 115 from national organisations, inter-university and non-university bodies (category C)
- 370 from groups within universities (category D)
- 107 from individuals (category E)

A Institutions on the UGC's grant list and the Northern Ireland universities

1. University College, Cardiff
2. (Superseded by A27)
3. Welsh National School of Medicine (now University of Wales College of Medicine)
4. The New University of Ulster
5. University of Wales Institute of Science and Technology
6. University of Manchester
7. University of Keele
8. University of Reading
9. University of Edinburgh
10. St David's University College, Lampeter
11. University of Strathclyde
12. Manchester Business School
13. London Business School
14. University of Exeter
15. University of Sheffield
16. University of Aberdeen
17. Brunel University
18. University of Glasgow
19. University of York
20. University of Wales
21. University of Durham
22. University of Newcastle-upon-Tyne
23. University of Lancaster
24. University of Bristol
25. University of Oxford
26. University of Manchester Institute of Science and Technology
27. University of Stirling
28. University of Technology, Loughborough
29. The City University
30. University of Leeds
31. University College of Swansea
32. University of Essex
33. University of Southampton
34. University College of Wales, Aberystwyth
35. The Queen's University of Belfast
36. University of Dundee
37. University College of North Wales, Bangor
38. University of St Andrews
39. University of Liverpool
40. University of East Anglia
41. University of Kent at Canterbury
42. University of Warwick
43. University of Hull
44. University of Bath
45. Imperial College of Science and Technology, London
46. University of Birmingham
47. University of Bradford
48. University of Leicester
49. University of Cambridge
50. University of Nottingham
51. University of Sussex
52. Heriot-Watt University
53. University of Salford
54. University of Surrey
55. University of London
56. University of Aston

B Vice-Chancellors and Principals of Institutions on the UGC's grant list

1. (Not used)
2. The City University — Vice-Chancellor
3. University of Sussex — Vice-Chancellor
4. University of Wales Institute of Science and Technology — Principal
5. University of Reading — Vice-Chancellor
6. University of Exeter — Vice-Chancellor
7. University of York — Vice-Chancellor
8. University of Kent at Canterbury — Vice-Chancellor
9. University of Technology, Loughborough — Vice-Chancellor
10. University of Surrey — Vice-Chancellor
11. University of Keele — Vice-Chancellor
12. University of Strathclyde — Principal and Vice-Chancellor

C National organisations, inter-university and non-university bodies

1. Medical Research Council
2. Standing Conference on University Entrance
3. Institute of Chartered Secretaries and Administrators
4. Joint Committee of Colleges of Education in Scotland
5. Society for Old Testament Study
6. Catholic Maintained Schools' Commission
7. Science and Engineering Research Council
8. Women's Engineering Society
9. Universities' Council for the Education of Teachers
10. British Universities Association of Slavists
11. London Mathematical Society
12. Conference of Heads of Departments of Geography in Universities of the British Isles
13. Association of Professors of Modern Languages in Technological Universities
14. RIBA Education and Professional Development Committee
15. Historical Association
16. Consortium of University Research Libraries
17. Girls' Schools Association: Education Sub-Committee
18. Royal Geographical Society
19. Scottish Examination Board
20. Engineering Employers' Federation
21. Institution of Electrical Engineers
22. Natural Environment Research Council
23. Parliamentary Labour Party
24. Royal College of Surgeons of England (Faculty of Dental Surgery)
25. Higher Education Foundation
26. Association of Scientific, Technical and Managerial Staffs (technician members)
27. Staffordshire County Council Education Committee
28. The Fellowship of Engineering
29. University Marine Biological Station
30. National Association of Teachers in Further and Higher Education
31. Conference of Representatives of Environmental Science in Universities of the United Kingdom
32. Association of South-East Asian Studies in the United Kingdom
33. Conference of University Administrators, Working Party on supplementary sources of income for universities
34. Scottish Business Education Council

35 Conference of University Administrators
36 Association of University Teachers (Scotland)
37 Society for Latin American Studies
38 Standing Conference of National and University Libraries
39 National and Local Government Officers Association
40 The Council of the Royal Society
41 Standing Conference of Professors of Physics in Universities
42 British Geomorphological Research Group
43 Economic and Social Research Council
44 Committee of Heads of University Law Schools
45 Institute of British Geographers
46 National Association of Head Teachers
47 Association of Integrated and Degree Courses in Nursing
48 Political Studies Association of the United Kingdom
49 Council of University Classics Departments
50 Institution of Chemical Engineers
51 Inter-University Committee on Computing
52 North-West Universities: Finance Officers Group
53 General Synod of the Church of England: Board of Education
54 United Kingdom Committee of Heads of Schools of Pharmacy
55 Council for National Academic Awards
56 British Dental Association
57 Association of Graduate Careers Advisory Services
58 British Society for the History of Science
59 Society for Research into Higher Education
60 National Union of Public Employees
61 Central Council for Universities Non-Teaching Staff: Trade Union side
62 Headteachers' Association of Scotland
63 British Academy
64 Society of Public Teachers of Law
65 Institute of Chartered Accountants of Scotland
66 Confederation of British Industry
67 Committee of Directors of Polytechnics
68 Biochemical Society
69 Association of Scientific, Technical and Managerial Staffs (academic members)
70 Headmasters' Conference
71 Committee of Heads of University Chemistry Departments
72 Council of Departments of Accounting Studies
73 (Not used)
74 National Council for Modern Languages in Higher and Further Education
75 Committee of Principals and Directors of the Scottish Central Institutions
76 Association of Learned Societies in the Social Sciences
77 British Medical Association Medical Academic Staff Committee
78 National Union of Students (Scotland)
79 Deans and other representatives of University Faculties of Arts and Social Studies
80 Social Democratic Party (Education and Training Policy Working Party)
81 Association of University Professors of French
82 British Psychological Society
83 Conference of University Convocations
84 Library Association
85 British Educational Research Association
86 Division of Community Affairs, British Council of Churches
87 Institute of Acoustics
88 British Computer Society
89 Association of University Teachers
90 Institute of Manpower Studies
91 Convention of Scottish Local Authorities
92 National Union of Students
93 Engineering Council
94 Committee of Vice-Chancellors and Principals
95 Liberal Party
96 Trades Union Congress
97 (Superseded by C106)
98 Heads of Scottish Law Schools
99 National Union of Students (Wales)
100 Scottish National Party
101 Huddersfield Polytechnic
102 Engineering Professors' Conference
103 Institute of Chartered Accountants in England and Wales
104 Development Studies Association
105 University Hospitals Association (Dental Schools)
106 Inner London Education Authority
107 Council for Educational Technology for the United Kingdom
108 Royal College of Veterinary Surgeons
109 Universities Group of the Association of Art Historians
110 Institute of Biology
111 Institution of Electronic and Radio Engineers
112 British Medical Association: Monitoring Body on the Effects of University Cuts on Medical and Dental Faculties
113 Association of Polytechnic Teachers
114 The Open University
115 Dental Education Advisory Council (Dental Schools)
116 Socialist Educational Association
E90 Committee of Directors of Dainton Courses

D Groups within universities

1	**Leeds**	School of Geography
2	**Manchester**	Departmental Board, Department of Social Anthropology
3	**Durham**	Board of Studies in Law
4	**Manchester**	Departmental Board, Department of Physiology
5	**London (Imperial)**	Department of Mathematics
6	**Durham**	Board of Studies in Politics
7	**AUT, (RHC, London)**	
8	**Manchester**	Departmental Board, Extra-Mural Department
9	**Manchester**	Department of History
10	**Manchester**	Department of Decision Theory
11	**Exeter**	School of Education
12	**(See end of Category E)**	
13	**Manchester**	Department of Government
14	**London (Birkbeck)**	Department of Geography
15	**Leicester**	Department of Religion
16	**London (Imperial)**	Computer Policy Committee
17	**Cambridge**	Masters and Fellows, Corpus Christi College
18	**Durham**	The Governing Body of St Chad's College
19	**Bristol**	Department of Extra-Mural Studies
20	**Manchester**	Faculty of Science
21	**Manchester**	Faculty of Economic and Social Studies
22	**London (RHC)**	Department of French
23	**London**	Warburg Institute
24	**Swansea**	Department of Geology
25	**Durham**	Faculty of Arts
26	**Heriot-Watt**	Video Course Services Advisory Board
27	**AUT (Manchester)**	
28	**Sussex**	Arts Area Career Tutors
29	**Oxford**	Institute of Social Anthropology
30	**Reading**	Department of Meteorology
31	**London (Imperial)**	Blackett Laboratory
32	**London**	Board of Studies in Law
33	**Bangor**	Board of Studies in History
34	**London**	Institute of Archaeology
35	**Queen's Belfast**	Department of Geriatric Medicine
36	**Liverpool**	Faculty of Arts
37	**Durham**	St John's College with Cranmer Hall
38	**Durham**	Board of Studies in French
39	**Sussex**	School of English and American Studies
40	**Bangor**	School of Education

41	Manchester	Manchester Museum		97	Loughborough	Department of Physical Education and Sports Science
42	Cardiff	Department of Electrical and Electronic Engineering		98	Liverpool	Senate Library Committee
43	AUT (Bristol)			99	Sussex	Chaplaincy Committee
44	London	Royal Postgraduate Medical School		100	AUT (City)	
45	AUT (Royal Veterinary College, London)			101	Swansea	Lecturers' Association
				102	London	Westfield College (see also D263)
46	London	Royal Veterinary College		103	East Anglia	Students' Union
47	Newcastle	Department of Fine Art		104	London	Computing Services (see also D378)
48	Liverpool	School of Educational Studies		105	Sussex	Committee of Deans of Science Schools
49	Cardiff	Faculty of Economics and Social Studies		106	Oxford	Wadham College
50	Manchester	Departmental Board, Department of Archaeology		107	Oxford	Students' Union
				108	London (Bedford)	Faculty of Arts
51	AUT (Keele)			109	Birmingham	Faculty of Education
52	Durham	Board of Studies in Oriental Studies		110	ASTMS (Manchester)	
53	Cambridge	Appointments Board		111	Loughborough	Ecumenical Christian Staff Group
54	Loughborough	Board of the School of Human and Environmental Studies		112	Cambridge	Faculty Board of Clinical Medicine
				113	Strathclyde	University Joint Unions Group
55	Manchester	Board of the Faculty of Education		114	London (RHC)	Department of Drama and Theatrical Studies
56	York	Some lay members of Council				
57	Swansea	Faculty of Education		115	Cardiff	Faculty of Science
58	Oxford	St John's College		116	AUT (Reading)	
59	Sussex	Education Area		117	AUT (Edinburgh)	
60	UWIST	Department of Psychology		118	Sussex	School of Engineering and Applied Science
61	Salford	Department of Sociological and Anthropological Sciences				
				119	AUT (Heriot-Watt)	
62	London	Institute of Child Health		120	Aberystwyth	Non-Professorial Staff
63	Cardiff	Faculty of Arts		121	NALGO (Leeds)	
64	Strathclyde	Department of Modern Languages		122	Loughborough	Research Committee
65	Sussex	School of Cultural and Community Studies		123	Durham	Board of Studies in Modern History
				124	City	Academic Staff Association
66	Oxford	Wolfson College (see also D91)		125	AUT (Cardiff)	
67	NALGO (Senate House, London)			126	Cardiff	Faculty of Education and Related Professional Studies
68	London	Board of Studies in Theology		127	AUT (London)	
69	Oxford	Board of Faculty of Biological and Agricultural Sciences		128	Loughborough	Board of the School of Pure and Applied Science
70	Keele	Board of Humanities		129	Loughborough	Department of Human Sciences
71	Salford	Department of Orthopaedic Mechanics		130	Oxford	Hertford College
72	Sheffield	Department of Chemistry		131	AUT (King's College, London)	
73	AUT (Bath)					
74	Sheffield	Students' Union		132	London	Institute of Psychiatry
75	WNSM	Non-Professorial Teaching Staff		133	Dundee	Labour Party Workplace Branch
76	Cardiff	Faculty of Applied Science		134	Surrey	Department of Educational Studies
77	Sussex	Arts and Social Studies Area		135	Oxford	Principal and Fellows of Somerville College
78	Oxford	St Hilda's College				
79	Aberdeen	Students' Representative Council		136	Reading	Faculty of Letters and Social Sciences
80	AUT (Surrey)			137	Bristol	Faculty of Social Sciences
81	ASTMS (Glasgow)			138	Sussex	Biochemistry Subject Group
82	Loughborough	Historians		139	AUT (QEC, London)	
83	Hull	Research Students' Association		140	London	Board of Studies in Mathematics
84	London	The Council: Chelsea College		141	Strathclyde	Bioengineering Unit
85	Manchester	Department of Community Medicine		142	Durham	Centre for Middle Eastern and Islamic Studies
86	Heriot-Watt	Students' Association				
87	Warwick	MA Applied Social Studies students		143	Cambridge	Research and Contract Group
88	London	Board of Philosophical Studies (see also D352)		144	Salford	Convocation
				145	UMIST	Students' Union
89	AUT (Aberystwyth)			146	Sussex	School of African and Asian Studies
90	Loughborough	Board of Studies, School of Engineering		147	NALGO (Sussex)	
91	Oxford	Wolfson College (addition to D66)		148	London	Board of Studies in Pharmacology
92	AUT (Essex)			149	Dundee	Department of Modern Languages
93	Keele	Lecturers' Association		150	Loughborough	Students' Union
94	London	Department of Extra-Mural studies (see also D375)		151	Manchester	Faculty of Arts
				152	Lancaster	Board of Studies D (Arts)
95	St Andrews	Business Committee of the General Council		153	Dundee	Department of Civil Engineering
				154	Swansea	Faculty of Arts
96	AUT (Library Sub-Committee, Sussex)			155	Leeds	Faculties of Arts, Economic and Social Studies, and Law

156	Leeds	Faculty of Science	214	AUT (Aberdeen)	
157	Leeds	Faculty of Engineering	215	York	Students' Union
158	Leeds	Faculty of Medicine	216	Keele	Students' Union
159	Leeds	Board of Collegiate Academic Awards	217	AUT (Cambridge)	
160	Sussex	Students' Union	218	Sussex	Graduate School in Arts and Social Studies
161	Glasgow	Department of Hispanic Studies			
162	London	Students' Union	219	Leeds	Department of Music
163	Durham	Students' Union	220	Edinburgh	School of Engineering Committee
164	Salford	Department of Geography	221	London	University College
165	Cambridge (King's College)	Students' Union	222	Bangor	Students' Union
			223	London	Royal Holloway and Bedford Colleges (see also D260)
166	Salford	Clifford Whitworth University Library			
167	Salford	Department of Politics and Contemporary History	224	AUT (UWIST)	
			225	Sussex	Science Studies Subject Group
168	Manchester	Departmental Board, Department of Geography	226	Hull	Students' Union
			227	Birmingham	Modern Languages Committee
169	Cambridge	Faculty Board of Economics and Politics	228	Glasgow	Faculty of Science
170	Durham	Some members of the Department of Economics	229	Newcastle	Students' Union
			230	London	Board of Studies in Zoology
171	Manchester/UMIST	Joint Departmental Board of the Metallurgy and Materials Science Department	231	AUT (Nottingham)	
			232	York	Board of Studies in Mathematics
			233	Cambridge	Churchill College
172	AUT (Chelsea College, London)		234	Bangor	Department of Philosophy
			235	Surrey	Academic Assembly
173	Keele	Chaplains	236	Bradford	Postgraduate School of Language and European Studies
174	AUT (Strathclyde)				
175	Bangor	Circle of Welsh Lecturers	237	Essex	Department of Sociology
176	Lancaster	Students' Union	238	Birmingham	Guild of Students
177	London	Birkbeck College (see also D255)	239	Durham	Junior Common Room of St John's College with Cranmer Hall
178	Manchester	Professors of Engineering			
179	Glasgow	Department of Zoology	240	Manchester	Faculty of Theology
180	AUT (St Andrews)		241	Leeds	Students' Union
181	Bradford	Students' Union	242	(Duplicate copy of D226)	
182	Birmingham	Department of Physics			
183	AUT (Birmingham)		243	Essex	Students' Union
184	St Andrews	Non-Professorial Staff Association	244	Aberystwyth	Faculty of Economic and Social Studies
185	Leicester	Students' Union	245	Loughborough	Department of Civil Engineering
186	(Included in D353)		246	Aston	Standing Committee of Academic Assembly
187	Birmingham	Faculty of Medicine and Dentistry			
188	London	Board of Studies in Botany (see also D327)	247	Aston	Library Staff
189	AUT (Sheffield)		248	Manchester	Department of Accounting and Business Finance
190	AUT (Belfast)				
191	London	Queen Mary College (see also D259)	249	Leeds	Department of Social Policy and Health Service Studies
192	AUT (QMC, London)				
193	London (QMC)	English Department	250	AUT (Lancaster)	
194	London (QMC)	Department of Civil Engineering	251	Durham	Joint Union Policy Committee for Non-Academic Staff
195	Edinburgh	Students' Association			
196	Aberystwyth	Guild of Students	252	Durham	Careers Advisory Board
197	Manchester	Students' Union	253	Bath	Students' Union
198	Nottingham	Students' Union	254	Cambridge	Chemical Engineering Syndicate
199	Bristol	Students' Union	255	(Included in D177)	
200	Aston	Guild of Students	256	London	King's College
201	Exeter	Guild of Students	257	London	The London School of Economics and Political Science
202	Sussex	Trade Union Liaison Committee			
203	Hull	American Studies	258	London	Queen Elizabeth College
204	Hull	Nursing Studies	259	(Included in D191)	
205	AUT (Hull)		260	London	Royal Holloway and Bedford Colleges (see also D223)
206	Leeds	Board of the Faculty of Education			
207	Aberystwyth	Cylch Darlithwyr CPC (Circle of Welsh Medium Teachers)	261	London	School of Oriental and African Studies
			262	London	The School of Pharmacy
208	(See end of Category E)		263	London	Westfield College (see also D102)
			264	London	Wye College
209	NUPE (Leeds University Branch)		265	London	Charing Cross and Westminster Medical School
210	AUT (Swansea)		266	London	The London Hospital Medical College
211	Cambridge	Faculty Board of Law	267	London	The Middlesex Hospital Medical School
212	Cambridge	Faculty Board of History	268	London	St George's Hospital Medical School
213	Cambridge	Faculty Board of English	269	London	St Mary's Hospital Medical School

270	**London**	United Medical and Dental Schools of Guy's and St Thomas's Hospitals
271	**London**	The British Postgraduate Medical Federation
272	**London**	London School of Hygiene and Tropical Medicine
273	**London**	British Institute in Paris
274	**London**	Courtauld Institute of Art
275	**London**	Institute of Advanced Legal Studies
276	**London**	Institute of Classical Studies
277	**London**	Institute of Commonwealth Studies
278	**London**	Institute of Education
279	**London**	Institute of Germanic Studies
280	**London**	Institute of Historical Research
281	**London**	Institute of Latin American Studies
282	**London**	Institute of United States Studies
283	**London**	School of Slavonic and East European Studies
284	**London (King's College)**	Faculty of Arts
285	**London (King's College)**	Faculty of Education
286	**London (King's College)**	Faculty of Natural Science
287	**London (King's College)**	School of Medicine and Dentistry
288	**London**	Careers Advisory Service
289	**(Not used)**	
290	**(Not used)**	
291	**AUT (Ulster)**	
292	**AUT (Hull: Brynmor Jones Library Staff Group)**	
293	**Brunel**	Students' Union
294	**London**	Board of Studies in Economics
295	**Wales**	Faculty of Technology
296	**Sussex**	Admissions Committee
297	**Cambridge**	Faculty Board of Classics
298	**Cambridge**	Faculty Board of Geography and Geology
299	**AUT (Newcastle)**	
300	**East Anglia**	Graduate Students
301	**Bath**	School of Education
302	**Bath**	School of Humanities and Social Sciences
303	**Bath**	School of Management
304	**Bath**	School of Modern Languages
305	**Bath**	School of Biological Sciences
306	**Bath**	School of Chemistry
307	**Bath**	School of Material Science
308	**Bath**	School of Mathematics
309	**Bath**	School of Pharmacy and Pharmacology
310	**Bath**	School of Physics
311	**Bath**	School of Architecture and Building Engineering
312	**Bath**	School of Chemical Engineering
313	**Bath**	School of Electrical Engineering
314	**Bath**	School of Engineering
315	**Bath**	Academic Assembly
316	**Bath**	Senate Committee on Educational Services
317	**Bath**	South West Regional Computer Centre and Computer Unit
318	**Bath**	Library
319	**London**	Academic Advisory Board in Engineering
320	**London**	Academic Advisory Board in Medicine
321	**London**	Academic Advisory Board in Science
322	**London**	Board of Studies in Agriculture and Horticulture
323	**London**	Board of Studies in Anthropology
324	**London**	Board of Studies in Architecture and Town Planning
325	**London**	Board of Studies in Biochemistry
326	**London**	Board of Studies in Biophysics
327	**London**	Board of Studies in Botany (see also D188)
328	**London**	Board of Studies in Chemical Engineering
329	**London**	Board of Studies in Chemistry and Chemical Industries
330	**London**	Board of Studies in Civil and Mechanical Engineering
331	**London**	Board of Studies in Classics
332	**London**	Board of Studies in Community Medicine
333	**London**	Board of Studies in Computer Science
334	**London**	Board of Educational Studies
335	**London**	Board of Studies in Electrical Engineering
336	**London**	Board of Studies in English Language and Literature
337	**London**	Board of Studies in Geography
338	**London**	Board of Studies in Geology
339	**London**	Board of Studies in Germanic Languages and Literatures
340	**London**	Board of Studies in History
341	**London**	Board of Studies in History of Art
342	**London**	Board of Studies in History of Science and Technology and Philosophy of Science
343	**London**	Board of Studies in Human Anatomy and Morphology
344	**London**	Board of Studies in Linguistics
345	**London**	Board of Studies in Medicine
346	**London**	Board of Studies in Microbiology
347	**London**	Board of Studies in Music
348	**London**	Board of Studies in Nutrition and Food Science
349	**London**	Board of Studies in Obstetrics and Gynaecology
350	**London**	Board of Studies in Oriental and African Languages and Literatures
351	**London**	Board of Studies in Pathology
352	**London**	Board of Philosophical Studies (see also D88)
353	**London**	Board of Studies in Physics (see also D186)
354	**London**	Board of Studies in Physiology
355	**London**	Board of Studies in Psychology
356	**London**	Board of Studies in Radiation Biology
357	**London**	Board of Studies in Romance Languages and Literatures
358	**London**	Subject Sub-Committee in French of the Board of Studies in Romance Languages and Literatures
359	**London**	Board of Scandinavian Studies
360	**London**	Board of Slavonic and East European Studies
361	**London**	Board of Studies in Social Administration
362	**London**	Board of Studies in Sociology
363	**London**	Board of Studies in Statistics
364	**London**	Board of Studies in Surgery
365	**London**	Board of Veterinary Studies
366	**London**	Board of War Studies
367	**London**	Special Advisory Committee in Areas Studies
368	**London**	Special Advisory Committee in Astronomy
369	**London**	Special Advisory Committee in Business and Management Studies

370	**London**	Special Advisory Committee in Drama
371	**London**	Special Advisory Committee in Ergonomics
372	**London**	Special Advisory Committee in General Practice
373	**London**	Special Advisory Committee in Geophysics
374	**London**	Special Advisory Committee in Human Communications and Speech Sciences
375	**London**	Council for Extra-Mural Studies (see also D94)
376	**London**	VTH Parry, DCLS and Goldsmiths' Librarian
377	**London**	Board of Studies in Archaeology
378	**London**	Computing Services (see also D104)
E22	**Durham**	Some members of the Department of Theology
E31	**Durham**	Boards of Studies in Engineering and Applied Physics and Electronics
E35	**Sheffield**	Ad hoc committee of academic and academic-related staff
E47	**London (Birkbeck)**	Department of Occupational Psychology
E58	**Birmingham**	Centre for Russian and East European Studies
E60	**Sussex**	Library
E102	**Glasgow**	Deans of the Faculties of Arts, Divinity, Law and Financial Studies, and Social Sciences

E Individuals

1	**Professor G G N Coles**	Chemistry and Geology, Oregon, USA
2	**A Gibson**	Philosophy/Biblical Languages, Cambridge
3	**Dr S M Bunt**	Anatomy, Dundee
4	**A Davey**	Applied Mathematics, Newcastle
5	**Professor O N V Glendinning**	Spanish, London (QMC)
6	**Professor J C Brocklehurst**	Geriatric Medicine, Manchester
7	**Professor A Sloman**	Artificial Intelligence and Cognitive Science, Sussex
8	**P A Gibbs-Kennet**	Director, Education and Professional Development RIBA
9	**Professor M G Whisson**	Social Sciences, Rhodes, USA
10	**Professor C V Brown**	Economics, Stirling
11	**Professor M Hammerton**	Psychology, Newcastle
12	**Professor R M S Smellie**	Biochemistry, Glasgow
13	**A R Gardner-Medwin**	Physiology London (UC)
14	**Professor J M Mitchison**	Zoology, Edinburgh
15	**Professor D Thorburn Burns**	Analytical Chemistry, Queen's Belfast
16	**Professor F E Dowrick**	Law, Durham
17	**Professor R A Weale**	Visual Science, London (Institute of Ophthalmology)
18	**W Lyons**	Moral Philosophy, Glasgow
19	**J Butterfield**	Philosophy, Cambridge
20	**Dr H P Rickman**	Philosophy, City
21	**Dr R H Roberts**	Systematic Theology, Durham
22	**(See end of Category D)**	
23	**Dr S P Chakravarty**	Economics, Bangor
24	**Professor T A Kletz**	Chemical Engineering, Loughborough
25	**Professor R E H Mellor**	Aberdeen
26	**Professor D A Wells**	German, Queen's Belfast
27	**Dr I Y Ashwell**	Geography (retired), Salford
28	**Dr D W Yalden**	Zoology, Manchester
29	**Professor H R Loyn FBA**	History, London (Westfield)
30	**Professor F Sawko**	Civil Engineering, Liverpool
31	**(See end of Category D)**	
32	**W B Woodward**	Science Librarian, Durham
33	**Professor P C Thonemann**	Physics, Swansea
34	**Professor I C Pyle**	Computing, York
35	**(See end of Category D)**	
36	**Professor J Duncan**	Mathematics, Stirling
37	**D H Roberts**	Technical Director, General Electric Co
38	**Dr S Clark**	English, London (Birkbeck)
39	**Dr J Herbert OBE**	Headmaster, Lliswerry High School
40	**Dr W I Kelso**	Biochemistry/Soil Science
41	**Dr C McCann**	Geology, Reading
42	**Professor P B Fellgett**	Cybernetics, Reading
43	**A L Norton**	Local Government and Administration, Birmingham
44	**D B Welbourn**	Engineer
45	**Dr R Riley**	Secretary, Agricultural and Food Research Council
46	**Dr D J Croome**	Architecture and Building Engineering, Bath
47	**(See end of Category D)**	
48	**D Nott**	Modern Languages/Education, Bangor
49	**T Brown**	Student, Newcastle
50	**Dr J F Dowler**	Chemical Engineering, UMIST
51	**W B Jepson**	Engineer
52	**Professor A M Ross**	Educational Research, Lancaster (see also E113)
53	**Dr R G Hannam**	Mechanical Engineering, UMIST
54	**Dr N Whiteley**	Visual Arts, Lancaster
55	**Dr J V Scott**	Computer Science, City
56	**Emeritus Prof P F Wareing FRS**	Botany and Microbiology, Aberystwyth
57	**S L Bragg**	Director in Industrial Co-operation, Wolfson Cambridge Industrial Unit
58	**(See end of Category D)**	
59	**Dr A R Michell**	Veterinary Medicine, London (RVC)
60	**(See end of Category D)**	
61	**Dr P V Bertrand**	Statistics, Birmingham
62	**Dr R F Mottram**	Physiology, Cardiff
63	**Professor P H Millard**	Geriatric Medicine, London (St George's Hospital Medical School)
64	**Sir Kenneth Dover**	Oxford (Corpus Christi)
65	**Dr A Tarrant**	Engineering/Home Economics, Surrey
66	**R E Maddison**	Lay member of Council, Kent
67	**Professor A C Rose-Innes**	Faculty of Technology, UMIST
68	**Dr F Oalf Thornton OBE**	Lay member of Court, Strathclyde
69	**A J R Veale**	Chairman, CAMPUS Trust, Salford
70	**I Milligan**	English, Stirling
71	**Professor N F Kember**	Physics, London (St Bartholomew's Medical College)
72	**Professor A C Wardlaw**	Microbiology, Glasgow
73	**Professor D B Wilson**	French, Durham
74	**Dr J B Slater**	Computing, Salford
75	**M G de St V Atkins**	Administration, Lancaster
76	**Sir John Barnes**	Vice-Chairman of Council, Sussex
77	**Dr B L Cohen**	Genetics, Glasgow
78	**Professor R E Thomas**	Business Administration, Bath
79	**Dr E Rudd**	Higher Education Studies, Essex
80	**W B Harland**	Geology, Cambridge
81	**G J Shire**	
82	**Professor A J Brown CBE**	Economics (retired), Leeds

83	**Dr K W H Glass**	Pure Mathematics, Queen's Belfast
84	**Dr J Pinsent**	Greek, Liverpool
85	**Professor P W Campbell**	Politics, Reading
86	**Dr P G Wright**	Chemistry, Dundee
87	**Professor W G van Emden**	French, Reading
88	**Professor I J Maddox**	Pure Mathematics, Queen's Belfast
89	**Professor P L Spedding**	Chemical Engineering, Queen's Belfast
90	(see end of Category C)	
91	**T Sprinks**	Mathematics, Essex
92	**Dr M Holcombe**	Pure Mathematics, Queen's Belfast
93	**Dr H W French CBE**	Chairman of Council, Loughborough
94	**Dr P S Noble**	French Studies, Reading
95	**Dr D F Binns**	Electronic and Electrical Engineering, Salford
96	**C Mar Molinero**	Operational Research, Southampton
97	**R W Ambler**	Adult Education, Hull
98	**Dr M J Jaycock** *et al*	Loughborough
99	**Professor J Creedy**	Economics, Durham
100	**Professor D Lane**	Sociology, Birmingham
101	**Dame Elizabeth Ackroyd**	
102	(see end of Category D)	
103	**Professor T R Miles**	Psychology, Bangor
104	**Dr J B Lawton**	Salford
105	**Dr D E S Stewart-Tull**	Microbiology, Glasgow
106	**J L M Trim**	Director, Centre for Information on Language Teaching and Research
107	**Professor S A Tobias**	Mechanical Engineering, Birmingham
108	**D A G Smith**	Headmaster, Bradford Grammar School
109	**I Stronge**	Student, Southampton
110	**Dr P M Fleetwood-Walker**	Director, Centre for Extension Education, Aston
111	**D Wyatt**	
112	**J D Wragg**	Director of Corporate Engineering Rolls-Royce, and Trustee of CAMPUS, Salford
113	**Professor A M Ross**	Educational Research, Lancaster (see also E52)
114	**Professor N J Graves**	London (Institute of Education)
D12	**Professor J B Goodenough**	Inorganic Chemistry, Oxford
D208	**Dr Claude Hepburn** *et al*	Loughborough

Annex C

Digest of replies to Circular Letter 16/83

The replies received in response to the Committee's Circular Letter 16/83 run, on a very rough calculation, to five thousand pages and one and a half million words. For this digest, the universities' replies (Category A) were first summarised and significant novel points made in other replies were then added. Not every shade of opinion is reflected: points are incorporated only if made by a sizeable representative body or by several individuals or departments. In fact, there is a large measure of agreement between individual staff members, departments and universities. The length of the digest for a question relates more to the diversity of views expressed than to the intrinsic importance or complexity of the question. In references to classes of respondents, "universities" means institutions on the UGC grant list, and "departments" means constituent academic parts of universities (eg, faculties and boards of studies as well as departments so called), including schools and institutes of the University of London. Respondents are not identified with the exception of major national bodies. Questions 1 and 2 in the Circular Letter are not digested because these asked each university what it would do in stated circumstances. For convenience each of the remaining questions is reproduced in full before the digest of the relevant responses.

Resources and student numbers

QUESTION 3

On the assumption of constant resource per student in real terms from 1990-91 to the end of the century, how should the higher education system as a whole cope with student numbers dropping by 15 to 20 per cent between 1989-90 and 1994-95 and remaining constant thereafter? What scope is there for reorganisation? Do you see mergers or other forms of association between universities and public sector institutions as desirable and practicable? What scope is there for greater collaboration? Should a significant number of institutions be closed during the five years 1990-91 to 1994-95? If so, what criteria and what machinery should be used to decide which institutions to close?

(1) Many respondents, either in answer to this question or in a general preamble, condemn the UGC's apparent acceptance of the Secretary of State's assumptions and initiation of consultation on that basis. One succinct expression of this view is: "The title, together with the claim that the document is inviting an 'open debate', is false because options for discussion have been limited by the stated premises. These already imply a policy with respect to both aims and resources; and this means that what is in fact being asked for is not a 'strategy' but merely tactics". The values underlying the assumptions are also criticised. For example: "The view of society adopted by the present government as it is reflected in statements by the Secretary of State for Education and Science and by the assumptions apparently underlying the (UGC's) questions, is that society is made up of individuals who are naturally competitive and properly concerned with the accumulation of wealth. Society as a whole is best served by encouraging the science and technology productive of wealth. This requires corporatist planning that . . . treats education as a commodity subject to market forces (based on employers' needs) rather than as a service to the community through the development and personal fulfilment of students at large. Such a position makes discussion of the future of higher education from educational and social perspectives difficult. But it is essential that these perspectives be maintained. Economic considerations are a necessary element in strategic planning but they should not be determinative. One . . . would hope that any consideration of educational strategy would not be restricted simply to the material benefits of an effectively educated society".

(2) Projections of student numbers. A large majority of respondents question the assumption of a drop in student numbers of as much as 15 to 20 per cent between 1989-90 and 1994-95, based on the DES's projections in Report on Education 99. Nearly all do so by referring to the projections prepared by the AUT, the CVCP and/or the Royal Society, and do not advance any additional evidence or critique of the projections. The factors repeatedly mentioned as insufficiently allowed for in the DES's projections are the changing social class composition of the population, the increasing participation rate for females, and candidates' preference for universities rather than public sector institutions. Less frequently mentioned are: demand from mature students, possibly fuelled by continuing high unemployment, which may also encourage staying on at school; a rising demand for skills in the later 1980s; and higher participation rates for social classes III, IV and V (encouraged in Scotland by proposed changes in school examinations), for the disabled and for ethnic minorities. Scottish respondents challenge the SED's projections. Reference is made to special factors in Northern Ireland, such as falling emigration. Two universities and a few others believe the case can be made for longer courses in some professional subjects. Those concerned with the subjects in question say that student numbers in medicine, dentistry and veterinary science are closely regulated by manpower needs and unlikely to be affected; that the demand for new recruits to school teaching will rise; and that demand will remain strong for graduates in various other vocational fields. Several respondents contest the view that postgraduate numbers should be planned as a function of undergraduate numbers, and believe that the need for vocational postgraduate courses will expand.

(3) Widening access. Many respondents argue that any spare capacity resulting from diminished demand from the "traditional" groups of university entrants should not be taken out of commission but should be used to extend participation among people who have not previously had the chance of higher education but could benefit from it and make a positive contribution to the cultural and economic development of the community. Positive measures should be taken to encourage groups mentioned in (2) and also to encourage greater participation from some regions. An economic justification for this lies in the low level of participation in tertiary education in the UK compared with our industrial competitors. One university observes that those admitted with relatively low academic qualifications show good rates of success, while another presses for more sub-degree courses in the public sector with a shift of degree students back into the universities.

(4) Diversifying provision. Many universities and departments think any spare capacity should be used also for new types of university education, both in the form of part-time courses which may be appropriate to the needs of groups mentioned in (3), and in the form of post-experience continuing education, the need for which is increased by rapid technological and social change. A couple refer to the impact on teaching methods of information technology, particularly in the form of distance learning. A few respondents prefer that any diminution in numbers of "traditional" entrants should be used to increase the time and support available to staff for research.

(5) Projections after 1995. Five universities say that the UGC's assumption of constant numbers after 1995 is wholly unwarranted, because even the DES projects a recovery.

(6) Resources. A few universities challenge the assumption about resources after 1990. First, many activities are unrelated to student numbers: services provided to constituencies outside the university in the form of libraries, museums and technical services; and also research and scholarship generally. Secondly, what would need to be done in response to falling student numbers at a constant unit of resource would depend on what the unit of resource was; and, in the light of recent experience, it is unrealistic to assume a constant unit of resource.

(7) Reorganisation. As most respondents do not believe that student numbers will, or should be allowed to, fall by as much as 15 to 20 per cent in the early 1990s, so they doubt that the need to reorganise institutions will arise. In general they support more collaboration between universities and with public sector institutions; they are sceptical of the benefits of mergers; and if student numbers really did fall so far, closure of some institutions would be preferable to the emasculation of all. Many answers are conditioned by an assessment of the university's local situation and, while acknowledging that collaboration, rationalisation, mergers and closures may be desirable or necessary, argue that one or more of the measures are not appropriate to that university. In appropriate cases, emphasis is placed on location (the university serves, and provides academic leadership in, a large

hinterland; other institutions are distant) and on size (the virtues of large institutions with a wide range of subjects and services, and of small institutions as more educationally effective, for many students. In relation to their own subjects, some departments nevertheless acknowledge that a few are too small and see rationalisation of provision as potentially beneficial, whether to give adequate expensive equipment or to protect minority subjects. London respondents refer to the reorganisation in progress, both to suggest that there is no more that can be done, and to predict that it will have been worthwhile. Librarians emphasise that only cessation of teaching and research in a subject can create significant savings, and make the case for even greater collaboration and for concentration of holdings.

(8) Collaboration. Universities and their departments say that much collaboration already occurs — between universities in research; and with neighbouring public sector institutions through validation of courses, in academic and non-academic services and, to a limited extent, in teaching. Most see scope for more collaboration, so long as it is academically beneficial, acceptable to the parties, and saves money. Emphasis is placed on achieving complementary patterns of activities. Some talk of rationalising overlaps in provision within a region, of complementary development in a locality, and of coordinating planning while maintaining diversity. Others warn against establishing regional structures, underlining the ability of universities, albeit autonomous institutions, to cooperate voluntarily.

(9) Mergers. Several universities' experience suggests that mergers entail considerable initial costs and accrue small recurrent savings, especially if split sites are involved. There may be some instances where nearby institutions overlap sufficiently in provision to merit consideration of merger, but to try to combine universities and polytechnics on a large scale would probably result in establishments in which the functions of neither would be effectively fulfilled: one large inferior institution could replace two smaller superior. To some, mergers would be no more than concealed or phased closures and should be avoided. Some universities report that they are currently engaged in discussions on mergers.

(10) Closures. If student numbers do fall, several respondents believe that degree courses in the public sector should be closed first. A widespread view is that closure of some universities would be preferable to dilution of all, as that would lead to none being able to maintain proper standards. Any such closures should be part of a reorganisation which protected educational opportunity. Few respondents consider criteria and mechanisms for closure, but the criteria suggested are typically the quality of teaching and research, student demand, and the need to retain a diversified and balanced system. As to who should decide, the UGC or a body independent of Government are proposed, but more respondents believe that the responsibility should clearly rest with the politicians.

Capital
QUESTION 4

How might any necessary reorganisation be financed from recurrent grant and proceeds of sale? Are the conditions which apply at present to the use of proceeds or any other rules relating to the use for capital purposes of resources from public funds unduly restrictive? If so, what changes would be helpful?

Most universities stress that large capital sums are needed to deal with the restructuring of the system and with obsolescence, and that funds for the maintenance of premises are inadequate. The current levels of recurrent grant leave little scope for financing capital projects, though, several argue, capital planning would be assisted by raising the present interchangeability limit of three per cent to five or six per cent or removing it altogether. Most consider capital-in-recurrent allocations too small to deal with the problems. Several criticise the unpredictability of the present *ad hoc* allocations and say planning would be assisted by more regular provision.

Several universities point out that the usefulness of the scheme for the retention of proceeds of sales varies from university to university, depending upon how much surplus property they have and how saleable it is. The general opinion is that proceeds of sales can never be large enough to fund major restructuring. Nevertheless most universities argue that the scheme should be made permanent and extended so that they are allowed to retain all proceeds. Some are prepared to see total retention subject to UGC approval. Most regard the present rules, where 50 per cent of sale proceeds over £100,000 have to be surrendered, as a disincentive to the sale of more expensive properties, and say that most of the smaller ones have been sold already. Some argue for the raising of the £100,000 limit, but most for total retention. A few are prepared to exclude newer buildings from this approach. Several want sale proceeds to be available for the purchase of equipment or to be used to endow academic posts. Universities find the time limits on the use of proceeds unduly restrictive and argue that they could lead to hasty and inefficient use of funds. Some seek a three year limit in all cases, others a four year, but most would like to see the limit removed altogether. Several universities argue for bridging finance and for long-term loans at low rates of interest.

Most universities press that they should be allowed to retain rents from grant-aided properties and point out that at present there is little incentive to spend money on the maintenance of unsaleable surplus property.

Of the comparatively few responses from other groups and individuals, most agree that proceeds of sales would be wholly insufficient to fund reorganisation. Several London colleges suggest that a powerful inducement to amalgamate would be the knowledge that capital released by the sale of one institution could be used to fund new buildings and equipment in the merged institution. The NUS and individual students' unions caution very strongly against stripping assets likely to be needed for longer-term developments, simply to release funds in the short term.

Balance of subjects
QUESTION 5

Does your experience suggest that there would be a demand for conversion courses? If so, how and in what kind of institution might it be appropriate to provide them? Can you see any other way of meeting the Secretary of State's wishes for a shift towards technological, scientific and engineering courses and towards other vocationally relevant forms of study?

(1) Many respondents question the desirability of a major shift in the balance of subjects towards engineering and technology, especially as it is difficult to predict the future demand for specific skills, with the possible exception of computing. A modest move towards "vocationally relevant" subjects, however, receives more general support (information technology is cited as an example of an area which has expanded rapidly in recent years) although many respondents insist that "vocationally relevant" is not synonymous with "technological, scientific and engineering". Indeed several arts departments report a demand for courses which inform scientists of developments in the humanities and social sciences, and others suggested that use of new technologies could be introduced across a wide range of disciplines. Other responses (including some from university careers services) question the demand for marginal candidates in the "right" subject as opposed to good candidates regardless of subject. There are considerable implications for libraries of any shift in emphasis to science and technology subjects.

(2) Pre-degree conversion courses attract little support. They are, at most, a short-term measure and can only be effective if offered to willing candidates. They are very expensive and may become a "soft option" for less able students. At least one conversion course has been discontinued because of the shortage of suitably qualified applicants. Conversions from arts to science are very difficult to achieve, especially in just one year although there may be some scope for more limited transitions. Nevertheless a few universities still run such courses or would be willing to do so if the demand existed and resources were made available. Several say the first year of their degree courses provides the opportunity for undergraduates to transfer between arts and science and a few suggest that a broader curriculum to first degree level would remove the need for remedial action in the form of conversion

courses. One or two respondents propose that certain core subjects be developed at undergraduate level irrespective of main subject. A common view is that conversion courses would be best offered by public sector institutions and should attract mandatory awards. One respondent suggest that courses could be provided on a regional basis by one university or college for the benefit of all universities in the area. In the long run, however, a permanent shift towards science can only be achieved by a greater emphasis on it in the school curriculum though there would be considerable implications for teacher manpower. The broader upper secondary curriculum in Scotland reduces the need for conversion courses. It is also necessary to improve status and career prospects, especially for women, in engineering and technology in order to attract the most able students.

(3) Postgraduate conversion courses. Those few universities which mention postgraduate courses strongly support the idea, and sixteen say they already offer a variety of courses at this level for which demand is high. However, any increase in the current level of provision to satisfy this demand is restricted by student number targets and postgraduate fee levels imposed on universities. Conversion is only feasible with adequate funds and staffing. A few universities are also in favour of mounting post-experience conversion courses for mature students, and other respondents suggest that these could be used to combat obsolescence.

QUESTION 6
Which subjects do you expect to become more popular, and which less popular, over the next decade?

The difficulty of predicting relative changes in the popularity of subjects is noted by a large number of universities. The factors which may influence student choice are many and almost all are impossible to forecast over a period of a decade. These factors include career perceptions; the curriculum and quality of teaching in schools; the effect of the increasing participation rate among women and the success of initiatives to encourage more of them to study science and engineering; technological advances which may result in the emergence of new areas of study; economic and social developments such as greater leisure; Government policies; and the action of universities themselves in creating new courses or improving existing ones.

Several universities decline to speculate about the future popularity of individual subjects while others limit themselves to suggesting possible growth-points within their own institution. Some universities emphasise the importance of developing existing courses to meet new needs, for example, the introduction of some computing into arts courses. Subjects which are identified as likely to become more popular across the system as a whole include computing, electronic engineering, information technology, some modern languages, biotechnology and some medical subjects, accountancy and business studies. Many universities think that high levels of unemployment will probably cause an increase in the popularity of courses which appear to offer the best career opportunities, but it is pointed out that it should not be assumed that vocational courses, narrowly defined, are necessarily the best preparation for work in a rapidly changing society.

Many subject-based respondents produce evidence of the continuing popularity of their own subjects, though there is also fairly widespread agreement with the above list. Several respondents are concerned that popularity should not be adopted as a criterion for supporting subjects, and suggest that popularity is immaterial.

Continuing education, in all subjects, appears likely to become more popular.

The need to maintain flexibility and a broad subject coverage within all institutions as the best way of responding to changes in student demand and national need is a theme in many responses to this question and to question 7.

QUESTION 7
Are there other reasons why you would wish to favour some subjects at the expense of others?

Universities say that they are concerned to preserve their essential nature as centres of learning each offering a broad range of subjects. They acknowledge that within that range there can be reasons for favouring some subjects from time to time. One consideration is the need to sustain the UK as a centre of science, culture and scholarship. On the one hand this may involve the need to strengthen basic disciplines, for it is from those disciplines that new subjects evolve; on the other hand it may require special protection for minority or currently unfashionable subjects in a few centres.

Some universities in Scotland and Northern Ireland emphasise the need for them to cover all subjects in order to preserve access to school-leavers in their countries. Similarly, in Wales it is thought necessary to protect Welsh, Celtic Studies, and teaching through the medium of Welsh.

Other reasons which universities think may justify favouring some subjects include the availability of careers for graduates; the extent to which a subject offers a flexible and rigorous intellectual preparation for life and work; the educational and research importance of a subject and its future prospects; national economic and social needs; and the strength of a subject in relation to other subjects in the same university and the same subject in other universities. A reason put forward by other respondents is the need to ensure an adequate supply of teachers across a wide range of subjects.

There is fairly widespread agreement among other respondents with the universities' comments and it is quite clear from their responses that arguments may be put forward for favouring almost all subjects. Many respondents, however, reject the suggestion that some subjects should be favoured at the expense of others.

Research
QUESTION 8
Do you think that in your institution the cuts of the last few years have fallen more heavily on research (and in particular on scientific research) than on teaching? Have you any quantitative evidence that bears on this question? If it has happened in your institution, are you taking, or do you intend to take, any counter-measures?

(1) Research and scholarship. Eight universities challenge the definition of scholarship in para 17 of the Circular Letter, asserting that the satisfactory pursuit of scholarship cannot be divorced from a concomitant involvement in research, that good scholarship is a prequisite for original research, and that research is an essential complement to university teaching in all disciplines.

Arts departments are the most critical, going so far as to suggest that scholarship has been so defined to legitimise the separation of teaching and research and to inculcate the view that research is pursued only in the natural sciences. They emphasise that their research is very cost effective and has only a tiny margin of non-salary expenditure of little use if transferred to science.

(2) Cuts have fallen more heavily on research than teaching? About half the universities answer clearly in the affirmative; many of the remainder are ambivalent, saying both have been hit; and only four definitely say not (but are clearly referring to the aggregate of general and specific expenditure). The majority refer to academic staffing falling faster than student numbers; to commitments to existing students and the need to sustain the teaching input if standards are to be maintained; to the administrative burden imposed (particularly on senior staff) by the implementation of cuts; and to the disruption of connected periods of time for research. Further increases in teaching loads are expected when part-time re-engagements end. Only two universities mention measures to reduce teaching demands, and another two the possibility of educational technology (with appropriate

initial investment) affording relief. The erosion of resources for research are exemplified by: a greater proportion of the remaining technicians being committed to the support of teaching; the loss of much technical expertise through retirements; cuts in consumables and travel budgets, library acquisitions, paid leave, and research posts financed from general funds; the insufficiency of the UGC equipment grant to enable obsolete items to be replaced by their (more expensive) successors, and the impossibility of supplementing it from recurrent funds; reductions in research studentships, particularly from the ESRC (but also, in some areas, the shortage of good home students because of poor career prospects); and the rising proportion of *alpha* rated applications which Research Councils cannot fund. In more qualitative terms, emphasis is placed on the loss of academic leadership in research as senior staff took early retirement and conversely the lack of stimulus from young colleagues, and a resulting slowing of tempo. The effects will not become clearly apparent for several years: thus a typical research project lasts for three years and publications appear two years later, while scholarly activity has protracted gestation periods, and only when the matter with which the scholar is already primed has been discharged will the lack of proper replenishment in the intervening period show.

(3) Counter-measures: external funding. Most universities say they have successfully redoubled efforts to raise more money for research from outside sources to cover shortfalls in UGC and Research Council funding, but they deplore how much staff time is absorbed by these efforts, and the shift towards short-term applied research to the neglect of long-term fundamental research. Departments are being of service to industry, but are diminishing their abilities to undertake research which in the longer term may be vital to the achievement of new products or processes.

(4) Counter-measures: internal resource allocation. Fourteen universities refer to the recent establishment of research committees with money to allocate in support of specified research projects, and a further seven refer to funds for pump priming. Three of these and three others have modified formulae and procedures for allocating general funds to departments so as to give greater weight to their research activities.

(5) Most students' unions and a couple of others say that teaching is the universities' primary activity, that too much attention is given to research in appointments and promotions, and that far more effort should be devoted to training university teachers.

QUESTION 9

Do you think that the dual support system can survive and would you wish it to do so?

(1) Advantages of the dual support system. All universities want the continuation of an effective dual support system, as the best system so far devised for the support of basic research. The reasons advanced are mainly those identified in the Merrison report. In particular, the university side allows: the maximum control of resources where it can most effectively and economically be exercised; support for unrecognised and speculative fields of research, and for young researchers to establish themselves; and new ideas to germinate anywhere within the universities. In the words of one university, the allocation from recurrent grant is like the "risk capital" of commercial enterprise, which produces growth. "University research groups must be permitted to cast a little bread on the waters; experience shows that much of it comes back after many days often buttered, sometimes on both sides." Multiplicity of sources of finance, both on the non-university side and as between it and the university side, minimise the errors of judgement on the promise of research. In several departments' view, peer group assessment is better than inexpert internal assessment for project funding. Only two respondents oppose the system, one proposing the transfer of the Research Councils' funds to the UGC.

(2) Making it effective. The universities are unanimous that the system is under strain but that it can survive if it is adequately financed on both sides. Several other suggestions are made. The UGC's funding of research should be (more clearly) complementary and responsive to each university's specific funding, and should allow for the overhead costs of applied, or contract, research. The Research Councils should reduce their international commitments, or at least funds for university research should be shielded from the fluctuations in exchange rates. Their in-house activities should be reduced, and their institutes should have to compete on equal terms with universities for funds. They should pay larger overheads. A Humanities Research Council should be established, especially as the arts subjects have growing needs for equipment and technical support, and as the British Academy is not an appropriate substitute. Interested departments say the current Council structure is inadequate for education, language teaching, law and nursing.

(3) Alternatives are discussed in terms of sources of funds other than the Research Councils. Industry is not seen as a dependable source of funds for basic research. In any case industrial funding varies geographically, according to the relative health of regional economies, and carries with it the risk of external prescription of research. For the social sciences, the other sources are nearly all themselves dependent on public funds, so not well placed to substitute for the Research Councils.

QUESTION 10

Would you favour earmarking, or indicating, the research component of the UGC grant? If so, what items of expenditure would be covered by this earmarking or indicating?

(1) Earmarking. The question did not define earmarking with any precision, but most universities seem to have assumed that within the block grant a single sum would be separated for the costs (or certain categories of costs) of all research met from general funds. One university is in favour, as are the science faculties in another. All others are opposed, on grounds such as that: the university's ability to deploy resources according to its perception of need, making use of detailed local knowledge, would be unacceptably limited; inflexibility in deployment of resources would be encouraged; sufficiently sensitive criteria could not be developed centrally because historical data would have to be used; teaching and research are inseparable in the work of the individual academic; greatly increased administration and meaningless bookkeeping would be entailed. However, a couple of universities say that the earmarking of the equipment grant has been valuable, and several more see no objection in earmarked grants for new developments. The Royal Society and a few others want the extension of this earmarking to include the basic costs of maintaining the well-found laboratory. A larger proportion of science than arts departments favour earmarking, though they usually interpret it as being by subject.

(2) Indicating seems to be construed as the same as earmarking, except that the university is not obliged to spend the stated sum on research, and is almost as widely opposed. But five universities see some merit in exploring its feasibility.

QUESTION 11

The Secretary of State has suggested that greater selectivity of research funding may be needed, both within institutions and between institutions. What are your views on this?

(1) Greater selectivity between institutions. Many universities pointed to the selectivity which already occurs through peer review in the Research Councils, and find that acceptable and adequate. Only a couple would welcome greater selectivity by the UGC on measurable criteria, though others accept the necessity of concentrating expensive facilities (which should be available to all) and of concentrating minority subjects. Generally there is opposition to creation of "centres of excellence" and of classes or tiers of institutions, especially if that meant some universities were designated as "non-research", as it is of the essence that university teaching should be informed by research, and as research excellence is found somewhere in every institution (and, so the smaller argue, is not concentrated in the larger). Staff contracts include the obligation to engage in both teaching and research, and a research base should be provided for all staff or at least all departments. Excellence is founded on individuals, and the opportunity

should be provided for it to emerge anywhere. Greater selectivity would lead to inflexibility and ossification. The Royal Society favours "centres of excellence" though not on a fixed basis, and a few science departments want more selectivity. Arts departments are generally strongly against, both because it is not needed in their subjects and because they fear it would drain resources away to other subjects.

(2) Greater selectivity within institutions. Only about a third of universities comment on, and all accept as necessary, greater selectivity internally, arguing (as in answers to earlier questions) that they are best placed to exercise discrimination and are developing mechanisms to do so.

(3) Research plans. The Secretary of State's letter of 1 September 1983 suggests that the UGC might allocate some funds only after joint consideration with the Research Councils of individual universities' research plans. This point is not made in the Circular Letter but is taken up by three universities, which say that it would be helpful if the UGC did consider their plans and priorities for research in broad terms and did indicate the extent to which those plans had been taken into account in determining the grant. The CVCP says that the universities would be prepared to examine such a system, and three Research Councils lend their support, expressing willingness to cooperate with the UGC. In a similar vein, a couple of other universities ask for fuller information on the factors taken into account and the formulae used.

QUESTION 12
What priorities, if any, would you suggest for special research investment (beyond those already identified, such as microelectronics, information technology and biotechnology)?

Almost all respondents say that it is essential to maintain a broad base of research covering all fields and that doing so should diminish the need for priority programmes. Any allocation of funds to priority areas of research should, therefore, be in addition to and not drawn from existing resources. Diversity in research is a necessary prerequisite for the development of new ideas since it is impossible to predict where the next new field of enquiry will occur and without a full spread of pure research endeavour there can be no certainty of initiating, identifying, or benefiting from the next development. Consequently, it is important that the definition of a priority area should not be too narrow or restrictive. There is some criticism of previous special programmes, including the recent information technology scheme, which have not always been well thought out or successful in achieving results. An evaluation of such initiatives is favoured before any further programmes are established.

Speaking in general terms, most respondents regard multi-disciplinary and inter-disciplinary research as priorities because it is difficult to attract support at present for such fields which are not usually covered by a single Research Council or grant-awarding body. To alleviate this problem there might be stronger links between SERC, NERC and ESRC through ABRC. A small minority of respondents suggest that more resources should be invested in the development of commercial products as a result of recent discoveries and innovations. Many universities name specific subjects for special investment most of which fall in the fields of: the social and economic effects of new technology; Third World technology; health science; environmental science; law and business studies; language teaching methods; computer applications in arts-based subjects; robotics; materials science; engineering and communications technology, and research relevant to local needs. Many arts departments regret the technocratic nature of the examples and suggest that no university system should ignore the arts and humanities. Another respondent comments that the examples are, in any case, all syntheses and extensions of basic disciplines.

Finally, one university feels too much money is being spent on "big physics" and astronomy and suggests that resources diverted from these fields could radically affect the development of other less expensive research activities.

Dependence on public funds
QUESTION 13
Are there respects in which you would wish your university to have greater freedom from the control of DES and UGC? What do you see as the financial advantages of this? And the non-financial advantages? What scope do you see for raising additional income, whether tied to specific purposes or not? Could the prospects be improved by a change in the tax laws? If so, what?

Universities recognise that their dependence on public funds properly involves public accountability and some measure of "control". Several say that costraints applied by the UGC are neither excessive nor unreasonable. Others point to ways in which they feel the Government of DES or UGC have encroached upon universities' autonomy in recent years, and regret this trend. Many respondents emphasise the need to restore sensible planning horizons and mechanisms, such as those which operated under the quinquennial system. The uncertainties of annual allocations make it difficult to plan and to use resources in the most efficient way.

A number of universities wish to have greater freedom to determine their own home student numbers and not to be subject to UGC targets. A few see merit in being allowed to set their own tuition fees, but as many are opposed to any changes in home fee arrangements which might restrict access or undermine the principle that entry to university should be based on academic merit. This latter view is supported by many other respondents. Other changes which some universities wish to see include greater virement between all types of expenditure; the inclusion of equipment grant allocations in general recurrent grant, with appropriate UGC guidance about their use; a reform of the present administration of student maintenance grants which they think is cumbersome and costly; a simplification of some UGC data collection and clarification of the Committee's grant allocation procedures; and consideration of the division of responsibility between the UGC and the Computer Board for funding computing facilities. Several universities comment here, or in their response to question 4, on the restrictive nature of rules governing the disposal or exploitation of capital assets. One university makes this point by commenting that Treasury rules appear not to have caught up with the Government's philosophy of encouraging entrepreneurial activities in the universities.

There is much opposition in principle to the substitution of private for public funding, and some respondents argue that the State has a responsibility to provide for education at all levels and for basic research. Others fear that the "greater freedom" of more private funding might actually result in more explicit controls by outside funding agencies, some of whom might not be sympathetic to the traditional values of a university in meeting the needs of society. Pressures to concentrate on subjects or research areas where funds can be raised would upset the balance of the university system and restric academic freedom. There is therefore unanimous belief that, in practice, it is inevitable that the Government should remain the main source of funds for universities.

In recent years every university has sought to raise more non-UGC income. Some have launched appeals and all have engaged in determined efforts to recruit more overseas students, to attract more research grants or contracts, to earn more from continuing education, and to strengthen their industrial and commercial liaison and consultancy work. Many think that there is further scope for raising income in these ways, but none believe that it is realistic to expect such income to replace public funding. Money from industry and commerce is normally tied to specific projects and almost never given to support basic research or teaching; it is liable to be cut off in times of economic recession; and its availability to any particular university will often depend on that university's location and subject mix. Industry needs universities that are sufficiently maintained to be credible recipients of funds for specific projects. Universities will therefore continue to be dependent on Government funds unless, as a few respondents suggest, the Government introduces a requirement (such as that apparently existing in Norway in respect of oil companies) that industry should fund basic research. Other respondents agree that a Government sponsored levy on industry would be a more sensible way to encourage research. An investigation into how industry and universities can work together more effectively may be advisable. A further commitment of staff to generating funds from other sources, particularly if this is unlikely to be commensurate with the returns, seems a misuse of academic resources. Private income would make no significant difference to the funding of libraries. Donations from individuals, including alumni, are highly valued by universities but they represent a very small proportion of total income. Most universities doubt whether they could be significantly increased except in the long term and as a result of a fundamental change in attitudes towards the private endowment of universities. Students' unions are adamant that current students should not be a target for providing additional income, whether through increased fees or through increased charges for services and accommodation, without commensurate increases in the student grant. Also, fund raising is unlikely to be successful if it is seen as a means of relieving the state from its funding responsibilities.

Many respondents believe that the prospects for raising additional income can be improved by changes in the tax laws, though one respondent suggests that it would take two generations to create the right climate and develop habits of charitable giving.

The nature of universities

QUESTION 14

Is there an essential difference in function between universities and other institutions of higher education, or should they be regarded as a continuous spectrum of institutions?

For nearly every university and department, the distinctive function of universities is their commitment to research, pursued in conjunction with teachig. Some emphasise the significance of teaching done in the context (or atmosphere) of research: universities are concerned to develop understanding of fundamental structures and processes so that known problems can be tackled in new ways and as yet unimagined problems approached, and only those engaged in research can conduct education of this kind. Consequential characteristics are identified: universities teach only at first degree level and above; they teach nearly all the postgraduates; they have national and international roles; their academic staff are contractually obliged to engage in research, and are afforded a high measure of autonomy.

University respondents who draw explicit contrasts with the non-university institutions characterise them as above all engaged in teaching courses specifically designed to reflect the opportunities and requirements of the (local and regional) employment market, with a variety of levels and modes of attendance, and disseminating well-established knowledge. Several question the polarity implied by the contrast, especially the suggestion that universities are not responsive to economic and social needs, whether national or local. But there is a more general concern that the distinction has been blurred, that the public sector institutions have run down sub-degree courses which particularly provide good training for technicians, and have ambitions to extend their research activities. In that there are spectra of institutions in both sectors, so there is in practice a continuous spectrum across higher education. Respondents speaking for public sector higher education emphasise the comprehensive range of its educational provision, its vocational orientation, and its teaching role. A widely held wish is to recognise differences in function, to afford those various functions parity of esteem, and to confirm the binary line by seeking complementarity of provision.

QUESTION 15

If there is an essential difference in the teaching function of universities and of other institutions of higher education, what is it, and how, in measurable terms, can one distinguish between those school-leavers who would benefit most from university type education and those who would benefit most from other types of higher education?

Following from the characteristics of a university education defined in answer to question 14, many university respondents see their teaching as aimed at students capable of self-direction and independent thought. Some go further to say that it is of the essence of universities that the ablest students of each generation are taught by the ablest scholars and researchers. Several refer to the HMI report on *Degree courses in the public sector of higher education* (1983) and infer that the factual and descriptive teaching with only limited analysis and independent learning, widely found in that sector, may suit students who, while capable of first degree work, lack the sustained analytic power of the very ablest undergraduates. University entrants have higher scores in A-levels and Scottish Highers, but these, the only available form of measurement, are imperfect as predictors of future performance — though found more adequate by science than arts departments. Those who pursue this line of thought further conclude that higher education must rely on self-selection by students, allied to good information and advice, careful admissions procedures, flexible entry criteria, and scope for transfers between courses. In fact, many school-leavers are capable of benefiting from a variety of types of higher education, and low wastage rates suggest that selection is not seriously defective. Some non-university respondents regret that the most able are automatically encouraged to make university their first choice.

QUESTION 16

Should there be more variety among universities in respect, for example, of disciplinary specialisation, type of student (mature, overseas etc), teaching style and involvement in research?

Three universities and several departments have answered "Yes" or "No" without explanation, but the remainder replying at length show a consensus on many points. Higher education is called upon to meet a great diversity of needs, and a wide variety of patterns of provision is required in response. Amongst the universities that variety already exists: considerable differentiation between institutions has evolved organically and is one of the system's strengths. It recognises that different universities excel in different ways at different times, and that as national and local needs change, as university personnel change and as subjects develop or lose their importance, the variety which is desirable changes. Institutional evolution should be allowed to continue without central direction to promote differentiation. As to the types of differentiation suggested, universities are clearest on involvement in research, consistently with their answers on questions 11 and 14: research is an essential function of all universities and mechanisms for selectivity already operate.

Respondents regard a good mix of types of student as both socially and educationally desirable, and in any case the actual mix reflects the disciplinary specialisation, the amount and type of residential accommodation, accessibility, and local social and economic characteristics. They envisage the mix becoming more diverse with the expansion of continuing education. The only support for differentiation by teaching style is with reference to sandwich courses because of the problems of arranging placements. Some acknowledge that specialisation by subject may be dictated by the expense of facilities or the limited demand for the subject, but they emphasise that a university should have a wide spread of disciplines because one of its strengths lies in the presence and interaction of expertise in many fields. Large and small universities argue the virtues of their own size.

QUESTION 17

Do you have views on a desirable balance in the university system, between provision for:

(i) **undergraduates, taught postgraduates and research post-graduates?**

(ii) **initial and post-experience provision?**

(iii) **full-time, sandwich and part-time provision?**

In what ways does your view of the desirable balance for your own institution differ from your view of the desirable balance for the system as a whole?

Universities consider that it is impossible to define precisely and for all time a desirable balance between modes and levels of provision in the university system as a whole. All types of provision should be represented in proportions which will vary over time according to factors such as demand, employment need, academic objectives and financial provision. The same is true for individual institutions and, indeed, for individual departments. The right balance for one will not be right for another with a different subject mix and sited in a different geographical location. There is a place within the system for institutions and departments which specialise, as well as for those which offer a full range of provision. The majority of universities and many departments say that the number of postgraduate students has fallen too low in recent years, following the cuts in Research Council and DES studentships and the increases in overseas student fees. Research postgraduates play a valuable part in the research function of the universities, in helping to maintain the intellectual vigour of academic staff and the discipline, and in providing a useful contribution to undergraduate teaching. Their numbers should be increased and should not be seen as a function of the number of undergraduates.

University respondents consider that more taught postgraduate courses are also needed, for vocational training and for professional updating, and in disciplines where specialist techniques cannot be covered adequately at undergraduate level. All universities endorse the importance of continuing professional education and most say that post-experience provision should be expanded but not at the expense of opportunities for school-leavers. Many universities are actively developing their involvement in continuing education and many others are preparing to do so. Inadequate financial support for students, as well as for institutions, is seen as an obstacle. Some universities acknowledge that their own involvement will be limited by geographical location and subject mix.

Subject mix and geographical location are also thought to be the major factor in determining the balance between full-time, sandwich and part-time provision. The great majority of universities have long-standing arrangements for part-time postgraduate study and many are now introducing part-time undergraduate degrees. As yet the level of demand is uncertain and is seen as depending on the size of the catchment area and whether provision exists in nearby public sector institutions. Universities which offer sandwich courses state their firm commitment to them but warn that an expansion of this mode of provision depends on the availability of good quality industrial and commercial placements.

Validation

QUESTION 18

What is your experience of the process of accreditation by professional bodies in those subjects in which they operate? What are your views on any other possible system of accreditation or validation of university courses?

The views expressed by inter-university organisations, academic staff groups and individual academic staff are generally similar to those of the universities, and that can be assumed unless stated to the contrary.

(1) Accreditation. The universities express general satisfaction with the process of accreditation though with many different shades of emphasis. The following two quotations encompass many of the points made by other respondents:

> "Accreditation by professional bodies of courses and examinations which confer a licence to practise is in principle justified and often plays a valuable role in inducing greater consideration of course structure, content and preparation... On the other hand, accreditation procedures can be time-consuming, can inhibit experimentation in teaching and forms of examination and assessment and may lead to a 'levelling down' in respect of academic work by imposing a minimum standard calculated according to easily measured dimensions such as contact hours or periods of practical experience."

> "Training for the professions requires liaison with professional bodies although it is essential that this liaison should be grounded in very substantial measures of university responsibility and academic freedom if flexibility and innovation are to be preserved and supported."

Emphasis is placed (i) on finding (and on the difficulty of finding) the appropriate balance between the influence of the two parties, between the practical and professional elements of a course and the academic and theoretical content; and (ii) on the benefits of a system of accreditation constructively designed by the professional body and imaginatively interpreted by the academic body. One respondent points to the value of accreditation visits for disseminating information on developments between institutions. Several universities point to the benefits for the professions: the former can exercise a moderating influence on the narrow views of some of the latter, and show the way forward to changes which a profession is slow to recognise as inevitable. Some professional bodies are considered to interest themselves in excessive detail, and the tendency to be prescriptive is seen as increasing. The more extreme view, expressed by the NUS, is that the accreditation process is often used to narrow and restrict courses so that they fit the orthodox model set by the professional bodies. Furthermore, attempts to exert pressure on the internal allocation of resources are unwelcome; or alternatively, the professions' demands cannot be met without extra resources unless there is to be a drain of resources away from courses which are not accredited. As one respondent observes, accreditation does tend to protect teaching against research when resources are reduced.

Comments are offered by a minority of universities, by relevant departments and by inter-university bodies on the process of accreditation for several named professions. The practices in medicine and dentistry (except at postgraduate level) are praised for the flexibility left to the univesity while maintaining standards. General satisfaction is expressed with the practice in accountancy, nursing and pharmacy. Opinions differ on psychology (but favourable in the majority), on law (critical in the main, particularly because of the attempts to expand the "core" subjects), and on social work (critical in the majority).

Architecture and planning, and computer science, each attract one adverse comment. Engineering is the profession attracting most comment, generally critical. Some feel that the Engineering Council has made a good start or cannot yet be judged, or that the situation has improved recently. But more refer to the highly specific (and sometimes conflicting) requirements of the various engineering institutions and to the difficulties of gaining accreditation for unified or combined engineering courses. Concern is expressed at the intrusion of Government represented by the proposed Council for the Accreditation of Teacher Education in England and Wales with members appointed and criteria determined by the Secretary of State who is also the provider of resources for training. Many would prefer an independent national body or local professional committees. The few accrediting bodies replying are satisfied that their own arrangements are not inhibiting for the universities. A few respondents say that accreditation should not be extended to further subjects (eg modern languages). One respondent feels that the professional bodies have failed to generate the training input to complement university education; and the CBI regrets their inflation of entry standards so as to close non-graduate routes to professional status.

(2) Validation of university courses. Academic staff are almost universally in support of the system of external examining as the means of monitoring the standard of university awards, and against the need for a national system of validation for university courses. Universities consider that external examining works well and cannot envisage any substantially different system which would work better while remaining consistent with universities' essential independence in the pursuit of academic excellence. One group make the additional point that without research as an integral part of the university's role in the subject taught, the process of self-validation would lack credibility. Several acknowledge that it may be necessary from time to time to make visible and convincing the existing means of monitoring standards; welcome the work of the CVCP group on academic standards;

and suggest how the external examiner's role can be reinforced by submission of written reports to the Senate or Vice-Chancellor and by being invited to assess courses critically. The two dissenting voices say that what little is known about the effectiveness of external examining is not encouraging, and that more stringent course development should be linked to enhanced activity in staff development.

Most academic opinion sees external validation on the lines of the CNAA's as expensive and bureaucratic, possibly encouraging rigidity and uniformity and inhibiting experimentation and continuous curriculum development. A couple of respondents point to the role of UGC sub-committees' visits in monitoring standards, but ask for better feedback. A few think there may be a case for a national inspectorial system.

The NUS, several students' unions and the SDP favour the extension of CNAA-type validation to the universities. It would guarantee the standard and quality of courses, which would be subjected to a more rigorous assessment and so a more thorough questioning of purposes and methods. It is also seen as a mechanism for extending credit transfer and modular course structures.

Tenure and premature retirement

The replies from many respondents to questions 19 to 23 reveal a deep concern for the problem of the unbalanced age distribution of academic staff and future levels of recruitment. The great majority emphasise the point that a regular intake of new academic talent is vital for the intellectual vigour and vitality of a university. Very few comment on the ABRC estimate that a replacement rate of 1¼ per cent is the least that can keep a science subject in good health, but one university that did think that 1¼ per cent is too low and suggests five per cent as a more realistic figure. A handful of universities point out that it is particularly important to preserve staff morale in a steady state or declining situation and in this respect they judge that the lack of promotion prospects is proving to be a serious handicap.

QUESTION 19

Would you favour the continuation of the new blood scheme? What do you see as its disadvantages and to what extent can they be overcome?

Most universities and departments see the new blood scheme as a short-term response to the financial problems of the last few years. They say that the scheme has been effective in supporting some areas of research in the sciences and has gone some way towards preventing the potential loss of a generation of young scholars. However, no university expresses unreserved support for the continuation of the scheme in exactly its present form and some respondents think that it should be ended immediately. The main disadvantages of the scheme are seen to be the undesirable extent to which it reduces a university's control over its own development; its time-consuming and cumbersome administration; the obscure criteria for the allocation of posts; the inadequate number of posts available and their uneven distribution as between the sciences and the arts; and the undue attention given to fashionable and sometimes narrow areas of research at the expense of the longer-term needs of universities as institutions and of mainstream teaching and research. Some respondents are also critical of the rules governing the scheme, particularly the upper age limit of 35 years which inhibits the recruitment of women wishing to return to work and of staff generally in areas where prior professional experience is necessary. The difficulty of having to rank applications from widely differing fields is also mentioned. One university suggests that the scheme should allow for part-time or fixed-term appointments; another considers that applications should be possible on behalf of actual persons as well as projects; and a third proposes that provision should be made for technical support staff. Some groups within universities, such as library staff, urge the extension of the new blood scheme to their areas of work.

The overwhelming view is that universities should be left to determine their own priorities for development in accordance with UGC guidance.

If, however, the new blood scheme is to continue it should do so for only a limited time and its funding should be additional to recurrent grant. Some respondents think that the UGC and the universities themselves should have greater influence than the Research Councils over new blood allocations and that those allocations should be part of a longer-term assessment of need rather than separate annual exercises.

QUESTION 20

What other realistic ways do you see of overcoming the problems of an unbalanced age distribution of academic staff and low staff replacement rates over the next five years?

Several respondents make the general point that most of the problems can be solved if the level of university funding is increased and secured for a reasonable period ahead. The majority, however, suggest specific schemes which might be considered assuming the hypothesis of a minimal or zero staff replacement rate. Over one half of the universities and a large number of others who responded to the question believe that exchange or secondment schemes should be developed. These might be between universities within this country or abroad or between universities and industry/commerce. Some central funding for such schemes is thought to be necessary to cover displacement costs, etc. Other suggestions include an expansion of continuing education and contract research work; the restoration of a UGC fund for restructuring; the raising of more non-UGC finance; a review of pension provisions to encourage mobility between university and other employment; a greater flexibility of employment including part-time, fixed-term, visiting and joint university/industry appointments; redeployment, retraining and study leave schemes; and the appointment of some high quality older academics to fill depleted age ranges. Many respondents also stress the importance of continued central funding of the PRCS and voluntary severance schemes.

QUESTION 21

Would you favour reducing the retiring age to 60, with the possibility of extending some academic staff beyond 60 on a non-tenured basis?

Opinion is fairly evenly divided on the question of a general reduction in the retiring age for academic staff to 60. Those opposed consider that it would be wrong to make retrospective alterations to current contracts of employment and they point out that universities need the experience of their older staff, many of whom retain their intellectual vitality at age 65 and over. Many of those in favour of a reduction in the retiring age see it as the best way of increasing the flow of new recruits. Virtually all universities, departments and individuals within universities in favour of a reduction say that their support is conditional on the preservation of the existing pension benefits. They point out that the cost of this would be high and there would be special problems in subjects where staff commonly enter university employment after a period working elsewhere. A number of respondents state that the age structure of academic staff in their institution, and across the system as a whole, is such that the retirement of all those over 60 will have only a marginal effect on the replacement rate during the next 10 years. There is general agreement that if the general retirement age was reduced to 60 extension beyond that age should remain a possibility in individual cases. A few respondents mention the need to keep the retirement age for clinical and non-clinical academic staff in line.

There is no opposition to the continuation of properly funded premature retirement and voluntary severance schemes. Many respondents think that such schemes offer the only realistic solution to the age structure problem provided they operate so as to allow for the replacement of staff who leave. The schemes would probably need to be centrally financed and universities hope that the Government would be prepared to make the necessary resources available.

QUESTION 23

Should the tenure provisions be the same in all universities? If so, what should they be? If not, would there be any long-term consequences?

The majority of universities say that tenure provisions should be broadly the same in all universities. The difference which exist at present, however, are not thought to have had any practical consequences although in an uncertain future it is thought that significant variations in tenure provisions would discourage staff mobility and work to the disadvantage of institutions with less advantageous terms. A number of universities state their firm opposition to enforced changes to their statutes.

Tenure provisions which prevent the termination of an appointment before normal retirement age, other than for good cause, are strongly defended by most universities as a way of protecting academic freedom and the long-term investment by individuals and institutions in their teaching, research, and scholarship. One or two universities think that freedom from dismissal solely as a means of protecting employment (as distinct from academic freedom) is difficult to defend. Several recognise that tenure is, perhaps, being granted too easily and too soon and they are in favour of a longer and more rigorous probationary period for academic staff. Some assume that any revised tenure arrangements could only be introduced for new staff and point to the undesirable dual standards which this would establish, to the difficulties of movement between institutions which it would create, and to the negligible practical effect that it could have before, say, the end of the century. One university which suffered a much greater than average cut in 1981 reports that despite the present tenure arrangements it has been able to arrange for well over 100 academic staff to leave in the last 2½ years.

Comments from departments are similar to those from the universities themselves. The AUT states that the removal of tenure would remove one of the main safeguards of academic freedom and points out that it is a privilege and responsibility which the academic profession cherishes and which it has been careful not to abuse. This is also the view of many academic staff groups. On the other hand some of the respondents from outside the universities express little sympathy for the concept of tenure. Tenure and its possible replacement is an issue on which there are strongly held views by individual respondents, both for and against.

The Leverhulme proposals
QUESTION 24
Would you favour the universal replacement of the present system of A-levels by a broader sixth form education and, if so, on what pattern? What would this imply for the quality and skills of your graduates?

QUESTION 25
Alternatively, would you favour making a broader sixth form education available to those who preferred it? If so, would you be willing to see your university's admission criteria altered so that students with a broader sixth form education were not at a disadvantage in applying for admission to your university?

Scottish respondents point out that the problems addressed by these questions are already catered for within the Scottish education system.

A majority of respondents are in agreement about the desirability, on general educational grounds, of a broader sixth form curriculum. Several make the point that the sixth form curriculum should not be viewed solely in terms of higher education but on its general educational merits, not least the effect on education before the age of 16. Many favour the universal replacement of the A-level system but without losing the opportunity for some study in depth. There is, therefore, support for combining a broader curriculum with the academic rigour of A-levels along the lines of the 1980 A/I-level scheme (anything resembling the earlier N- and F-level proposals would not meet with much support). Several respondents suggest patterns for a broader curriculum and there is a broad measure of agreement that elements of both the sciences and the arts should be included. There is some support too for the introduction of a common core of subjects to be taught in a broader curriculum, and for some standardisation of syllabi. One or two respondents say that A-levels are the best measure of attainment available.

Many respondents find it difficult to comment on the implications of change in the sixth form curriculum for the quality or skills of their graduates without knowing exactly how the curriculum might be changed. However, there is considerable support for the view that longer degree courses might be needed if standards are to be maintained. On the other hand, some respondents believe that an A/I-level structure would have no adverse effects on the quality of entrants to degree course; indeed a few universities already allow other qualifications such as the International Baccalaureate. Some respondents suggest that a broader sixth form curriculum may lead to pressure for increased participation in higher education.

Some respondents to question 25 say they would welcome an optional broadening of the sixth form curriculum as a step in the right direction and that admissions criteria should be adjusted accordingly. However, the majority think that it would be very difficult to cater fo two distinct levels of entrant. They believe that a broadening on this basis would be bound to fail because some departments would tend to favour the more specialised applicant and school children would be unwilling to take risks with their chances of entry.

The NUS and individual student unions call for mandatory student grants for all post-16 studies.

[N.B. Replies to the Circular Letter were received before the publication in May 1984 of the Government's consultative document on AS-Levels.]

QUESTION 26
Would you favour a change from present course structures to a sequence of two year modules?

Respondents are virtually unanimous in their opposition to two year degrees. They say that the present three year course has withstood the test of time and, in general, no convincing educational arguments have been presented for changing it. The three year course is already short by international standards and in some subjects, like engineering, the trend is towards longer courses. Two years is thought to be too short a time to assimilate and integrate the knowledge and skills required for a degree; at least three years is needed for students' intellectual maturation. Respondents say that two year degrees would be regarded as inferior by students and by employers and that it is unlikely that they would satisfy the requirements of professional bodies. They believe that there is unlikely to be much demand for two year degrees and one university which already provides an ordinary degree of BSc to be taken in two years reports that it is an option followed by few students. Many respondents say that to shorten the degree course at the same time as broadening the sixth form curriculum would be a disastrous combination. It would be illogical to expect students to proceed directly to a specialist course from a broader sixth form base, and in these circumstances an introductory module might be useful. It would of necessity, however, lengthen the degree course.

The only basis on which many respondents say they would support two year modules would be if the norm was for students to take two such modules. Many acknowledge that this would be expensive and therefore probably unrealistic. They also point to the need for any such change to be introduced simultaneously in all universities to facilitate transfer. Support for two year modules with the possibility of credit transfer rests on the flexibility that these introduce.

QUESTION 27
Would you favour a change in the structure of university courses in England and Wales, to offer a choice between a two year general degree and a three year honours degree, along the lines of the present structure in Scotland, or indeed, any other changes in degree format (including a longer academic year)?

Many respondents replied to questions 26 and 27 in combination, and the unanimous opposition to two year degree courses, and the reasons for it, are noted above. They point out that the comparison with Scotland is incompletely drawn, as the Scottish system rests on a minimum of three years study. It would be wrong to suggest that the structure of three years for the ordinary or pass level and four years for the honours degree could be reduced to a two and three year system. No degree course worthy of the name could be completed within two years. The Scottish system was established and thrives in a different environment. In part because the ordinary degree is often followed by a one year vocational diploma course (eg for school teaching), there is a ready market for its holders. South of the Border there is no such regard for general degrees. The UGC's Circular Letter is seen as confusing the distinction of general and specialised courses on the one hand, and pass (or ordinary) and honours degrees on the other. Several universities are willing to explore a three and four year structure on the assumptions of extra resources and a broader sixth form curriculum.

Respondents are opposed to a longer academic year for students, in the sense that they might receive formal teaching during more weeks of the year and might therefore complete existing courses of study in a shorter time. Already undergraduates in medicine, dentistry and some other vocational subjects are in formal attendance for nearly the whole year. Many other students use the vacations for fieldwork, projects, industrial and other forms of placement. Furthermore, even if teaching and these activities could be compressed into a shorter period, the students' intellectual maturation would be prejudiced because that required time. Lengthening the teaching year for academic staff without compensating increases in the number of staff, is also opposed, because it would erode the time available for research and other activities besides teaching. Universities point out that during vacations some staff teach, and plant is used for, short and in-service courses. There would also be severe implications for university libraries both in terms of stock and staff. A couple of universities acknowledge that the pattern of the academic year might be reviewed with advantage.

As regards other changes in degree format, one university looks for a more systematic approach to credit transfer, and a couple of others think that some four year courses might be made more modular.

QUESTION 28

Have you any comments on the role and nature of the UGC, or on the way in which it should carry out that role?

(1) Almost every university supports the continued existence of the UGC without fundamental changes to its constitution and working methods. The universities refer to the need for an intermediary to "reconcile the interests of the State as paymaster and the requirements of national policy with the proper academic freedom and autonomy of the universities". The UGC is seen as probably the best available mechanism for allocating resources between the universities and certainly better than any group of permanent civil servants. But the UGC has been exposed to political pressures that threaten its traditional independence. It has appeared unduly to accede to Government wishes and to take decisions without adequate consultation or explanation. Furthermore, inconsistencies of UGC policy in recent years have not improved the confidence which universities have traditionally placed in it. A few go further to say that the UGC's influence is too pervasive and inhibiting; and that it has failed to ensure that plans for university development are adequate to national needs, and to represent the universities to Government. Its standing in relation to the DES and the civil service in general has never been lower. Some accept that a Government committed to reducing public expenditure will seek greater control on how it is spent, and conclude that the UGC is then all the more necessary, but that, if it is to undertake a more active coordinating role, modifications to its composition and operations are necessary. University departments and staff are generally more critical (and trades unions and branches even more so) of the UGC's recent record, saying that it has become an arm of Government and has lost the confidence of those whom it is meant to represent.

(2) The UGC's role. The UGC should be seen to ascertain and to put the universities' view more explicitly to Government. It should more frequently express views independent of those of Government, and generally increase its distance from Government. It should be accountable to the general public and to the university sector as a whole.

(3) Membership. With one exception, the universities accept that members should be appointed by Government because much public money is involved, though possibly after wider consultation. But those appointed from universities should more fully reflect the diversity of the university system; and what is asked of them should attract the ablest individuals who should not only be distinguished academics but also well-informed and up to date about the system. Members should serve shorter terms but give a larger proportion of their time. A couple favour the inclusion of non-professional staff, senior university administrators, and/or experienced lay officers. Others want a larger non-university, non-educational, element on the UGC. The Labour Party, the TUC, the AUT and branches, a few departments, and one university want the UGC (or a Universities Council) to be a representative body, with members appointed by the Secretary of State, by the universities, by recognised trades unions, and by other interests such as the CBI. Such a body should have a much more open and accountable style of operation than the UGC currently has.

(4) Relationship with Government. It is generally agreed that the UGC should try to avoid further erosion of its authority. One means to that end would be for it to be more open in its advice to Government and to make that advice public. A contrary view is that, if the UGC were more distant from the DES, the DES would need a separate means of ensuring that the public interest was satisfied. The Chairman's right of access to the Secretary of State is valued. Several universities want the UGC's affiliation to the Treasury reinstated; another proposes the Privy Council and the Cabinet Office; yet another suggests regular reports to a select committee of the House of Commons as a means of public accountability.

(5) Relations with universities should be closer. If members and officers spoke freely to Vice-Chancellors and senior university officers, then the adversarial tone which has crept in would be dispelled. Many universities and nearly all constituent parts want more open discussion of the criteria which underlie the UGC's decisions; fewer ask for more information on the grant calculation. The CVCP, though, emphasises the confidentiality of each university's day to day dealings with the UGC. There are also requests for greater precision in the expression of intentions and policies, for written feedback after main and sub-committee visits, and for smaller, more frequent visits, in place of visitations. The few references to the sub-committees are to the effect that they are necessary and, if anything, should be made more effective; some doubt whether they give sufficient coverage of all subjects. The Scottish universities propose a Scottish sub-committee. One university proposes a regular academic audit of each university by a visiting panel not wholly drawn from the UGC's membership.

(6) Secretariat. There is repeated reference to the UGC office being insufficiently staffed to support the tasks expected of the UGC. It should be strengthened in calibre, numbers and expertise, so that there are sufficient resources to enable the UGC to take the initiative in formulating policies. Recently the staff turnover has been too rapid, and knowledge of the internal operation of universities is inadequate. Some universities propose the severing of the staffing connection with DES, so as to allow a more genuinely independently minded staff. Many advocate appointments (including senior ones) from universities, and also from other Government departments with relevant interests (eg DHSS, DTI), Research Councils and professional bodies. Several say that the UGC's data base and use of information technology should be improved. Advocates of a Universities' Council see an independent secretariat as an essential corollary.

QUESTION 29

Do you favour a proposal that a single body should be set up to take over some or all of the work of the UGC and, for example, NAB and the Wales Advisory Body, either replacing them or standing between them and Government, and if so in what form? More generally, do you see centralised coordination of both sectors as either desirable or feasible?

All but one university and nearly all departments answering are opposed to both a combined body and an overarching body. The reasons advanced are usually that the nature, functions, financing and governance of the two sectors are clearly distinct and warrant different treatment; and that a body embracing all higher education would be so large and wide-ranging as to be unable to determine and act upon priorities and would tend to reduce all institutions to uniformity. "Centralised coordination" is generally opposed on the grounds of having the same effects, but several universities stress the desirability of transbinary consultation and dialogue. In its most positive form these are seen as involving collaboration in collecting data, joint submissions to DES on questions of strategy, and a joint secretariat with staff on long-term appointments, not just from the civil service. The NUS, most students' unions, and NALGO want a regional structure of bodies responsible for all post-compulsory education in the long term, and reform of UGC membership and procedure in the short term. NATFHE calls for genuine transbinary planning at regional level. The Liberal Party and the Committee of Directors of Polytechnics favour an overarching body, while the SDP thinks a Royal Commission should review the structure of higher education. Scottish respondents outside the universities favour a combined or overarching body for Scotland.

Annex D

Comments on statistical projections of student numbers

THE PROCESS OF STATISTICAL PROJECTION

1 We must first say something about the process of statistical projection. In this process there are four stages. The first is to obtain data relating to the past behaviour of the system, eg student numbers to be projected. The second stage is to build a model for the behaviour of the system — that is, an explicitly defined deterministic process, which will in general involve a number of variables or parameters. Examples of such variables in our case are the size of the 18 to 19 year old cohort; the qualified participation index (QPI) which is defined as the number of home initial entrants aged 20 and under to full-time and sandwich higher education in a given year divided by the number leaving schools and further education establishments in the previous academic year with at least two GCE A-levels (three SCE Highers in Scotland); the social class mix of qualified school leavers etc. The model aims to provide a realistic approximation to those aspects of the real world that are being studied. The third stage is to state assumptions on the projection into the future of the variables which are used in the model. The purely arithmetical fourth stage is to feed these parameters into the model to obtain statistical projections.

2 The figures thus obtained are the model's projections of what will happen given the assumptions about future values of the variables. Often the calculations are repeated with different values of the key variables to produce alternative projections. The highest and lowest of the projections thus obtained are inevitably called the upper and lower projections, though that phrase can be misleading.

3 There can be discrepancies between the projections and what actually happens. A model is bound to be much simpler, as well as more deterministic, than the actual world; indeed, model building will always be an art as well as a science, and there will always be controversy between competing modellers as to the merits of their respective models. Controversy is fuelled, and decisions made harder, by the fact that models are seldom explicitly described by those who produce them; the model usually has to be deduced from the details of the calculations based on it. Moreover a model should assume no changes except those explicitly taken account of; but in practice many models have unstated policy objectives built into them.

4 Statistical information about the present and recent past is often unreliable or even unobtainable. Sometimes estimates have to be used instead of information, or surrogate information has to be used about a different but supposedly related phenomenon; sometimes the lack of data even forces the replacement of one model by a different one for which the necessary data are available.

COMMENTS ON PREVIOUS PROJECTIONS

5 The comments which follow take no account of the 1983 DES projections, since they are superseded by those of 1984. The DES, the Royal Society (RS), the CVCP and the AUT project different statistics and use different models. The most noteworthy difference is that the DES project demand for higher education as a whole, whereas the other bodies project numbers in the university sector alone. This distinction is fundamental in comparing the projections because the division between the universities and the public sector is a matter of policy, not one of statistical projection. Other differences between projections are that those of the DES and the CVCP relate to Great Britain whereas the others relate to the United Kingdom; the DES and the CVCP use Universities Statistical Record new entrants figures whereas the others use Universities Central Council on Admissions (UCCA) candidates or entrants statistics; all four bodies produce projections of new entrants but only the DES and the CVCP use these to produce projections of total student numbers; age groups examined vary from three by the DES to none by the RS; the AUT and the RS confine themselves to undergraduate projections, whereas the DES and the CVCP include postgraduate and overseas students.

6 There are further differences and clearly direct numerical comparisons are not meaningful. Conversion of the projections to index numbers does enable comparisons to be made of what each projection implies in terms of the relationship of past to future trends. The lowest trends in the 1990s are then those of the RS projection, followed by the DES projection and the first AUT projection. The high group comprises the second AUT projection and that of the CVCP. The Scottish Education Department also produced projections in December 1983, both for Scottish Entrants to higher education in the United Kingdom and for numbers of students in higher education in Scottish institutions.

7 The RS and the AUT use social class data from UCCA. These data are notoriously suspect; moreover, since nothing analogous is available for entrants to public sector institutions, both bodies are thereby committed to projecting university numbers rather than numbers for higher education as a whole. Most non-mature students who wish to enter higher education would prefer a university place to one in a public sector institution; demand for university places is therefore not a helpful quantity to estimate since that demand will certainly not be met. The university projection that is of interest is how many applicants will reach some pre-assigned level of qualification in each year. It is natural to take that level as the actual level of admission in some particular year.

8 The resulting figures can be used in two different ways. They can be used to estimate the number of university places that should be provided. For this it is important which year is used as a baseline since admission standards have been rising for some years, and have recently risen even more sharply because of the drop in the total number of university places. Indeed, if the same standard of entry had been applied in 1982 as in 1979, some 11,000 additional students would have been admitted to universities in 1982. Alternatively, it can be argued that trends in these figures should be the same as trends in the demand for places in higher education as a whole, so that projections for the latter can be derived from projections for the former by scaling up.

9 The AUT make two projections. The first is based on the same model as the RS but using statistics from a later year; this produces small changes, which can be regarded as a measure of one component of the uncertainty inherent in the process of statistical projection. The second projection also takes account of the continuing rise in the proportion of women in universities, and assumes that the proportion will reach equality by the 1990s. As an aim we applaud this, though it would seem to be more a policy than a projection. Unfortunately, the model underlying the AUT's second projection implicitly assumes that the male/female ratio in universities is the same in each social class. This is not a matter on which we have any data, but it seems so unlikely as to disqualify the model.

10 The CVCP model took account of the results of the RS model and is noteworthy in two respects. First, in participation indices, it allows for the fact that non-mature students do not all enter university at the age of 18; this correction smooths the projections, and has been incorporated into the latest DES projection. Second, it allows for some lowering of the standard of admission to universities. This has the effect of shifting some potential students from the public sector to the university sector.

11 A central problem in projecting student numbers is how to take account of social class and, in particular, class mobility. This is a notoriously controversial problem, made worse by the unsatisfactory nature of some of the statistical data. For non-mature students, the major difference between the DES model and that of the RS lies in their treatment of social class. A further central problem is taking account of female participation rates.

12 The DES are concerned with projecting demand for courses in higher education as a whole. In their calculations they require data on attainment

69

rates by social class (ie percentage of cohort in each social class obtaining two or more GCE A-levels or three or more SCE highers) of a kind which are available for Scotland but not for the rest of Great Britain; they therefore extrapolate the pattern for Scotland to Great Britain as a whole. This is an example of what is referred to above as the use of surrogate information. It is the only practicable way forward; but clearly it is not wholly satisfactory.

13 The contribution of the Royal Statistical Society's working party is largely to propose standards which any subsequent projections and their expositions should meet. We do not agree with all its proposals; for example it proposes that projections should be made separately for the universities and the public sector, with which we disagree for reasons given in para 5. Nevertheless any subsequent workers will have to give serious consideration to what it says. It puts forward its own view of future demand in a single concluding paragraph which is unconnected with the rest of the paper; the derivation of this paragraph is not clear, and it does not meet the methodological standards which the working party itself proposes. We do not think it deserves detailed consideration.

FURTHER ASPECTS

14 If the projection of student demand makes use of current figures for the number of places available, then it relies on the assumption that the number of places available is at present adequate to meet demand — in other words, that the Robbins principle is still being followed. The only way of testing this hypothesis which is available to us is to compare the number of applicants to universities (as recorded by UCCA) with the number of entrants to higher education. There are considerable difficulties in interpreting the results of this comparison, but it is an indicator that should not be ignored.

15 There is also the mysterious drop in the QPI for higher education as a whole since 1981 (87.8 in 1981-82, 86.0 in 1982-83, and 81.4 provisionally in 1983-84). The number of students entering higher education cannot exceed the number of places available, and one explanation of the drop is that the number of places available in the last few years has not been as great as the qualified demand. The number of places in the university sector has fallen as a result of the 1981 cuts, though the number of places in the public sector has risen in that period and not all of them have been filled. There is some evidence that there are significant numbers of well-qualified school-leavers who wish to enter a university but do not wish to enter a public sector institution. That would account for the drop in the QPI but implies that the Robbins principle is no longer being met. However, another explanation is that the QPI is affected by such things as the level of student grant (which has fallen in real terms) and the comparison between job prospects now and possibilities in three years' time. The QPI plays an important role in the DES model, and is involved in the scaling up of the other projections. Its variation over the next few years will be of considerable interest.

Annex E

Projections of university academic staff numbers

INTRODUCTION

The imbalance in the age structure of non-clinical academic staff in universities is described in para 7.2. In particular, the number of staff in the 35 to 49 age group represents too high a proportion of the total when compared with a balanced age structure, and the group aged 50 and over represents too low a proportion (although the 50-54 age group is roughly in balance). The implication of this is that in the normal course of events, the number of academic staff leaving university employment will for the remainder of the present decade remain below the level at which recruitment is needed to sustain the intellectual health of the university. If academic staff numbers remain constant, the actual number of recruits will be equal to the number leaving; if staff numbers drop it will be less. This is why it is suggested in para 7.5 that the level of recruitment is unlikely to be more than about 700 non-clinical academic staff a year, averaged over the remainder of the decade. This represents about 2.6 per cent of the total non-clinical staff whereas the proportion should be at least 3.5 per cent — that is, 900 a year — for a population of the present size. These conclusions are based on consideration of recent data and four projections of how the age distribution of non-clinical academic staff could change over the next fifteen years. This Annex describes those projections and their underlying assumptions.

BASE FIGURES AND ASSUMPTIONS

2 USR (Universities' Statistical Record) statistics of staff populations are recorded at a snapshot date of 31 December. For the purpose of measuring intake (new recruits to university service or staff returning after a period in other employment) or outflow (members of staff leaving university service), USR statistics reflect activity in the calendar year preceding the snapshot date, ie 1 January to 31 December. The latest year for which information is available from USR is 1982. Using the 1982 data, an age distribution of the estimated 1984 staff total has been constructed as a baseline for the four projections. For all ages, the constructed baseline takes account of information available to the UGC about net staff reductions, including staff leaving on premature retirement terms, between December 1982 and December 1984. Resignations, etc, of staff under 50 or over 63 have been assumed to continue at approximately the levels observed in recent years. For staff aged between 50 and 63 the historic rates have been replaced by the premature retirement figures plus 0.5 per cent of each age group (to allow for retirement through ill-health and death in service). The derived 1984 baseline age distribution of staff is shown in Appendix 1 column a.

3 This baseline age distribution is common to all four projections. The development of the four projections then depends on a combination of assumptions about:

(i) the total number of staff in the system in each future year;

(ii) staff losses for each age level in each future year;

(iii) the age distribution of recruits to the system.

The total number of recruits in any year is determined by assumptions (i) and (ii).

4 A constant number of staff was assumed for each projection except for Projection 3. Outflow rates for Projections 1 and 3 were the same, but different rates were assumed for each of Projections 3 and 4. A common age distribution of recruits to the system was assumed for each projection and for each future year; it was based on the observed age-distribution of recruits in 1979-80 and is shown in Appendix 1 column b.

PROJECTION 1

5 Projection 1 assumed a constant total number of staff for all future years. The outflow rates for each age level are shown in Appendix 1 column c. These were derived from the rates observed for 1979-80; small adjustments were made where, after comparing them with similar rates for 1980-81 and other years, there appeared to be anomalies at particular age levels in the 1979-80 rates.

6 The overall outflow rate produced by this projection is shown in Appendix 2 table B. It rises steadily from 3.1 per cent in 1984-85 to 5.1 per cent in 1999-2000. This steady rise results from the change in the age distribution, with which higher resignation and retirement rates operate. Total recruitment increases in line with the rising number of retirements and resignations and table 1 below summarises the changing age distribution over time of the total number of staff as produced by this projection.

Table 1 Projected staff numbers by age band assuming constant numbers overall and outflow rates and inflow distributions based on those observed in 1980.

(Thousands)

Age Bands	Dec 1984 No	Dec 1984 %	Dec 1989 No	Dec 1989 %	Dec 1994 No	Dec 1994 %	Dec 1999 No	Dec 1999 %	Steady State %
Under 30	1.2	4	1.4	5	1.6	6	1.9	7	7
30-34	2.5	9	2.0	7	2.3	9	2.8	10	12
35-39	4.8	18	2.9	11	2.5	9	3.0	11	13
40-44	5.7	21	4.7	18	3.0	11	2.8	10	14
45-49	5.2	19	5.5	21	4.7	18	3.1	12	15
50-54	3.5	13	4.9	18	5.3	20	4.5	17	14
55-59	2.4	9	3.2	12	4.5	17	4.9	18	13
60+	1.5	6	2.1	8	2.8	10	3.9	15	12
TOTAL	26.8	100	26.8	100	26.8	100	26.8	100	100

(Numbers may not total exactly due to rounding)

7 A steady state distribution is included in the final column of the table as a yardstick against which to assess the actual and projected age distributions. It is defined as the distribution of staff into age groups within a constant total which would ultimately be reached if the assumed normal recruitment (inflow) and leaving (outflow) rates were applied indefinitely, ie it is the age distribution which, when normal inflow and outflow rates are applied each year to a constant total number of staff, remains unchanged from year to year. Comparing the distribution of staff in various years against the steady-state distribution shows the imbalance in age groups. It shows in particular that the size of the 35-49 age group is, at the 1984 level of 58 per cent of all staff, very much greater than the steady-state size, for which the proportion is 42 per cent.

8 From table 1 it will be seen that the numbers in the age range 55 and above increase from 15 per cent of total staff in 1984 to 33 per cent in 1999. This shows the increasing capacity for recruitment of, in particular, young staff towards the turn of the century if it is assumed that the total number of staff remains constant.

9 The relatively high level of recruitment in the short term implied by Projection 1 was not in accord with the experience of UGC members (leaving aside the effect of the "new blood" recruitment) and the effect of modifying the outflow rates was therefore examined.

PROJECTION 2

10 Projection 2 assumed a constant total number of staff for all future years, as did Projection 1, but the effect of lower outflow rates was examined by assuming rates for each age level that were 25 per cent lower than those in Appendix 1 column c for all ages of staff except those aged 60 or over. The results are given in Appendix 2 table B. The overall outflow rate rises from 2.4 per cent in 1984-85 to 4.5 per cent in 1999-2000. The recruitment

levels that resulted from this projection were thought to be closer to reality than those from Projection 1, but the assumed outflow rates were thought to be below what would probably happen in practice. Before considering an alternative outflow assumption, the effect on recruitment of reducing the total number of academic staff was examined.

PROJECTION 3

11 Projection 3 assumed the same outflow rates as Projection 1 (shown in Appendix 1 column c) but the total staff numbers were assumed to fall by 1.5 per cent each year. The results are shown in Appendix 2 table B. The overall outflow rate rises from 3.1 per cent in 1984-85 to 5.5 per cent in 1999-2000, very similar to Projection 1 for the years up to 1994-95. The number of recruits is much lower than for Projection 1, ranging from 424 in 1984-85 to 636 in 1994-95. The assumption adopted for the reduction in total staff numbers was considered to be higher than was realistic for a properly managed system (it implies a reduction of approximately 2,000 staff in this decade alone) but it illustrates the damaging effect on recruitment levels of a falling staff population.

PROJECTION 4

12 The contraction in the size of the university system imposed over the last three years has disrupted the previous pattern of retirement. Any academic staff aged 50 and over who are still in post will have been under considerable pressure to take early retirement (and this probably applies even more strongly to those aged 55 and over). It is therefore uncertain how many of those who do remain will decide to leave before retirement age. Projection 4 assumed that those staff who were aged 50 and over in 1984 would not leave in the near future except at retirement age (or where retirement because of ill-health, or death in service, occurs). Outflow rates for this age group used in Projection 4 are shown in table 2 below. They are based on figures for death in service as recorded in the USR, increased by 50 per cent to take account of staff leaving on ground of ill-health. The outflow rates for staff aged 60-63 are substantially higher than those attributable to ill-health and death in service because they allow for women and some men retiring at those ages. For staff aged under 50 or over 63, the outflow rates are those shown in Appendix 1 column c.

Table 2 Outflow rates based on death in service and ill-health retirement: staff aged 50–63

Age	Outflow rate (%)
50	0.36
51	0.39
52	0.45
53	0.54
54	0.63
55	0.72
56	0.81
57	0.90
58	0.99
59	1.08
60	3.3
61	3.3
62	3.3
63	3.3

13 Operation of this model involves the progressive discarding of the outflow rates shown in table 2 above, starting with the lowest age, and replacing them with the appropriate rate from Appendix 1 column c. After 14 years, the rates shown in table 2 will have been totally replaced by those from Appendix 1. However this model is intended only to represent the short term (till 1990); results after that year are not considered to be reliable. Results given in Appendix 2 are shown up to 1999-2000 for completeness only. The changing age distribution over time is shown in table 3 below.

Table 3 Projected staff numbers by age band assuming constant numbers throughout and outflow rates and inflow distribution based on those observed in 1980 but adjusting rates by death/ill-health rates.

(Thousands)

Age Bands	Dec 1984 No	Dec 1984 %	Dec 1989 No	Dec 1989 %	Dec 1994 No	Dec 1994 %	Dec 1999 No	Dec 1999 %	Steady State %
Under 30	1.2	4	1.2	4	1.5	6	2.2	8	7
30–34	2.5	9	1.8	7	2.1	8	2.8	10	12
35–39	4.8	18	2.7	10	2.3	8	2.8	10	13
40–44	5.7	21	4.7	17	2.9	11	2.5	9	14
45–49	5.2	19	5.5	20	4.6	17	3.0	11	15
50–54	3.5	13	4.9	18	5.3	20	4.5	17	14
55–59	2.4	9	3.5	13	4.5	17	4.8	18	13
60+	1.5	6	2.6	10	3.8	14	4.2	16	12
TOTAL	26.8	100	26.8	100	26.8	100	26.8	100	100

(Numbers may not total exactly due to rounding)

14 Projection 4 shows overall outflow rates below those for Projection 1 until about 1994-95. These rates, and the implied levels of recruitment, are considered to be consistent with actual levels experienced recently.

SUMMARY AND CONCLUSIONS

15 The model which seemed most consistent with UGC members' experience of what has happened in recent years was Projection 4. Assumptions underlying this model were thought to be justifiable up to the end of this decade. Beyond that, it was considered that rates of retirement and resignation might return to a normal level more rapidly than this model implied. They might well be at the level of those experienced in 1982 (Appendix 1 column c).

16 The results of Projection 4 shown in Appendix 2 table B indicate that the average level of recruitment till the end of this decade is likely to be about 700 members of staff per annum, or about 2.6 per cent of a population of 26,800. The steady state inflow appropriate to a population of that size with a balanced age structure would be about 1,150 recruits per annum, or about 4.3 per cent of the total. This alone is not a sufficient indicator of the appropriate level of recruitment because the steady state represents a long-term ideal. Actual recruitment rates in 1978-79, 1979-80 and 1980-81 were 4.7 per cent, 3.5 per cent and 2.7 per cent respectively. 1978-79 marked the end of the period when universities were still planning for expansion, and 1980-81 was the first year in which many if not most universities had to cut back on recruitment because of the loss of income that resulted from the Government's new policy on overseas student fees. The recruitment rate in 1979-80 of about 3.5 per cent of the total number of staff can therefore be taken as a realistic level of recruitment at which to aim. Even in that year, the higher age groups represented a smaller proportion of the total than the steady state figure, so the levels of recruitment that were possible were below what was required for a balanced age structure, and 3.5 per cent represents a minimum figure. Applied to a total number of non-clinical academic staff for 1984-85 onwards estimated to be about 26,800, it produces a recruitment level of 900 per annum.

Appendix 1 to Annex E

Age	a Baseline age distribution of staff at December 1984	b Distribution of total inflow among age levels (based on 1980 data) %	c Outflow rates for Projection 1 as a proportion of each age level %
Under 25	110	9.0	11.5
25	150	9.0	11.0
26	200	9.0	9.5
27	232	9.0	9.0
28	245	7.0	8.5
29	297	6.0	6.6
30	365	6.0	4.5
31	465	6.0	4.0
32	485	5.0	3.8
33	570	5.0	3.6
34	662	4.0	3.1
35	821	3.0	2.6
36	864	2.5	2.3
37	1,073	2.0	2.1
38	1,026	2.0	1.9
39	1,023	1.5	1.6
40	1,164	1.5	1.3
41	1,237	1.5	1.3
42	1,155	1.0	1.3
43	1,064	1.0	1.3
44	1,081	1.0	1.3
45	1,082	1.0	1.3
46	1,180	0.75	1.3
47	1,039	0.75	1.3
48	978	0.75	1.3
49	873	0.75	1.3
50	797	0.75	1.5
51	732	0.75	1.6
52	692	0.5	1.8
53	710	0.5	2.0
54	580	0.5	2.1
55	528	0.25	2.4
56	512	0.25	2.6
57	475	0.25	3.0
58	458	0.125	3.4
59	378	0.125	3.6
60	371	0	11.0
61	286	0	11.0
62	278	0	11.0
63	226	0	11.0
64	200	0	11.0
65	77	0	50.0
66+	76	0	80.0
Total: 26,817			

Appendix 2 to Annex E

TOTAL NUMBERS, OUTFLOWS AND INFLOWS FOR NON-CLINICAL ACADEMIC STAFF

Table A — Actual Figures

Year	Total Numbers[1]	Outflows	Outflow rate	Inflows
1978–79	29,510	1,071	3.6%	1,397
1979–80	30,029	1,122	3.7%	1,053
1980–81	30,066	1,164	3.9%	815
1981–82[2]	29,715	2,164	7.3%	466

[1] Total numbers minus outflows plus inflows does not necessarily equal next year's total numbers for technical reasons — recategorisation, inter-university transfers, etc.

[2] 1981–82 was the first year of operation of the premature retirement scheme.

Table B — Projections

Year	Total Numbers	Outflows	Outflow rate	Inflows
1. BASE RUN: CONSTANT TOTAL NUMBERS, STANDARD OUTFLOW RATES				
1984–85	26,817	826	3.1%	826
1989–90	26,817	962	3.6%	962
1994–95	26,817	1,128	4.2%	1,128
1999–2000	26,817	1,354	5.1%	1,354
2. OUTFLOW RATES FOR UNDER 60s REDUCED BY 25%				
1984–85	26,817	645	2.4%	645
1989–90	26,817	795	3.0%	795
1994–95	26,817	964	3.6%	964
1999–2000	26,817	1,196	4.5%	1,196
3. TOTAL NUMBERS FALLING BY 1.5% per annum				
1984–85	26,817	826	3.1%	424
1989–90	24,865	868	3.5%	495
1994–95	23,055	982	4.3%	636
1999–2000	21,377	1,166	5.5%	845
4. OUTFLOW RATES FOR 50–63 GROUP REDUCED				
1984–85	26,817	642	2.4%	642
1989–90	26,817	831	3.1%	831
1994–95	26,817	1,112	4.1%	1,112
1999–2000	26,817	1,584	5.9%	1,584

Annex F

UGC EQUIPMENT GRANTS TO UNIVERSITIES

£m	1972-73	1973-74	1974-75	1975-76	1976-77	1977-78	1978-79	1979-80	1980-81	1981-82	1982-83	1983-84[2]	1984-85[2]
As provided — historical costs[1]	26.3	29.6	17.3	35.6	23.9	32.1	35.2	45.1	68.0	68.1	74.6	74.8	79.8
Revalued to January 1984 prices	93.0	98.6	46.2	77.6	45.1	52.7	54.2	60.9	82.2	76.2	77.8	74.8	76.0
Model-based calculation, January 1984 prices[3]	103.5	90.0	100.5	104.2	108.6	100.4	101.6	103.0	106.6	96.9	92.3	97.8	96.1
Accumulated deficit January 1984 prices	10.5	1.9	56.2	82.8	146.3	194.0	241.4	283.5	307.9	328.6	343.1	366.1	386.2

Notes:

[1] The figures relate to the equipment element within the combined furniture and equipment grant.

[2] The model-based calculation takes into account the initial and continuing provision of equipment associated with the IT posts.

[3] The model-based calculation does not take any account of the increase in inventory values resulting from the annual application to these values of the factors for development, change, and Research Council input. If the cumulative effect of this had been reflected in line 4 of the table, the total deficit in 1984-85 would have been close to £600m.

UGC EQUIPMENT GRANTS TO UNIVERSITIES: January 1984 prices

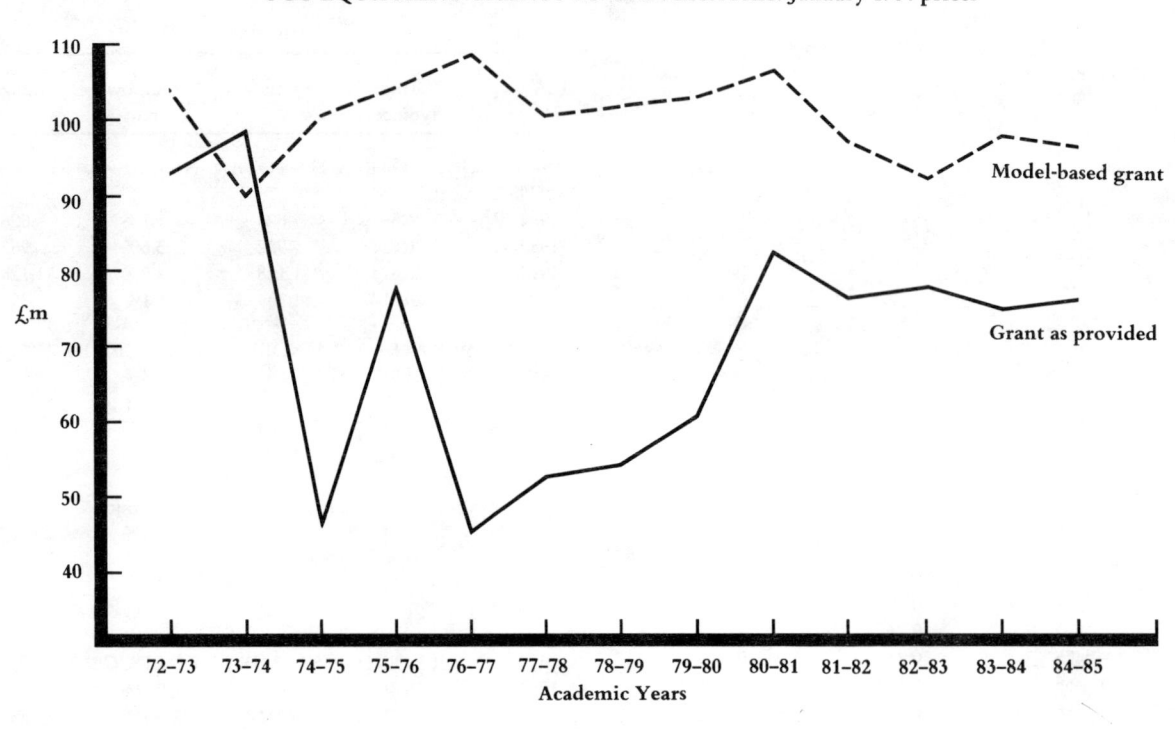

Annex G

Statistical tables

As a general background to the UGC's advice, the tables in this Annex give a selection of statistics for students and staff over recent years. With the exception of Tables 7 and 8, they relate to institutions on the UGC's grant list, ie they do not include the Northern Ireland universities or the Open University.

LIST OF TABLES

1. Student numbers (full-time and sandwich) — home and overseas.
2. New entrants (full-time and sandwich) — home and overseas.
3. Student numbers (part-time) — home and overseas.
4. Home student numbers (full-time and sandwich) — subject of study.
5. Home student numbers (full-time and sandwich) — arts, science, medicine.
6. Continuing education.
7. UCCA — applications and acceptances (United Kingdom).
8. A-level mean scores of new home entrants (full-time and sandwich) — England and Wales.
9. Student : staff ratios.
10. Age distribution of academic staff in GB universities: 1982-83.

GREAT BRITAIN

Annex G: Table 1

STUDENT NUMBERS (FULL-TIME AND SANDWICH) — HOME AND OVERSEAS

THOUSANDS

	1972–73	1977–78	1979–80	1980–81	1981–82	1982–83
HOME AND OVERSEAS TOTAL	239	281	293	299	300	295
of which: Undergraduates	193	232	245	251	253	250
: Postgraduates	46	49	48	48	47	45
Taught	22	25	24	25	25	24
Research	24	24	23	22	22	21
HOME TOTAL[1]	218	245	258	268	272	268
of which: Undergraduates	185	215	228	236	240	237
: Postgraduates	33	31	30	32	32	31
Taught	16	16	16	17	18	17
Research	17	15	14	14	14	14
of which: Men	148	156	159	163	164	159
: Women	69	89	99	105	108	109
Women as percentage of total	32%	36%	38%	39%	40%	41%
OVERSEAS TOTAL[1]	22	35	35	31	28	27
of which: Undergraduates	9	17	17	15	14	13
: Postgraduates	13	18	17	16	15	14
Taught	6	9	9	8	8	7
Research	7	9	9	8	7	7
OVERSEAS TOTAL as percentage of all students	9%	13%	12%	10%	9%	9%

(NUMBERS MAY NOT SUM DUE TO ROUNDING)

[1] Based on fee-paying status. From 1980–81 onwards, home numbers include, and overseas numbers exclude, students from European Community Countries (1981–82 for students from Greece).

GREAT BRITAIN

STUDENT NUMBERS (FULL-TIME AND SANDWICH) — HOME AND OVERSEAS

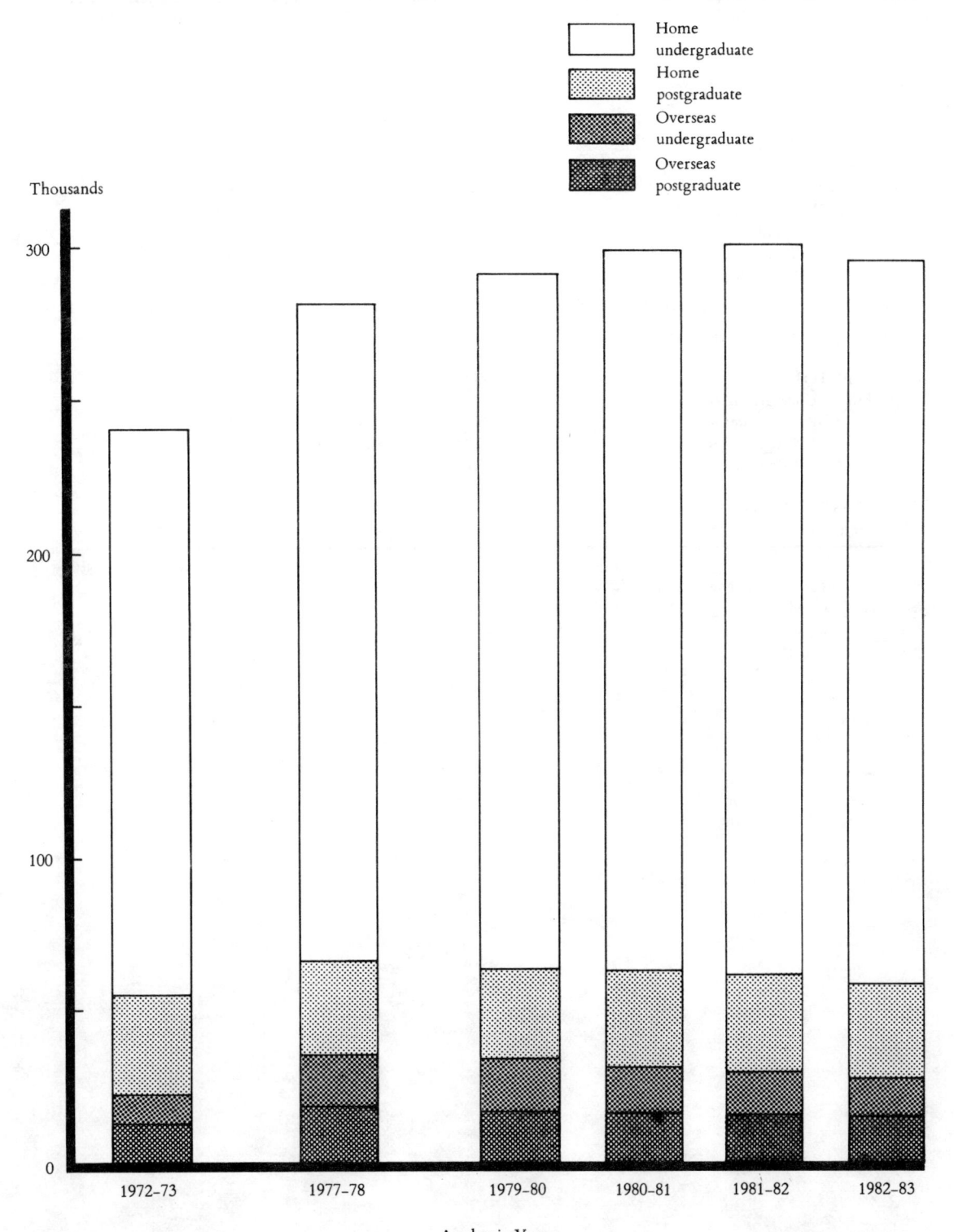

□ Home undergraduate
▨ Home postgraduate
▩ Overseas undergraduate
▧ Overseas postgraduate

Thousands

Academic Year

GREAT BRITAIN

Annex G: Table 2

NEW ENTRANTS (FULL-TIME AND SANDWICH) — HOME AND OVERSEAS

THOUSANDS

	1972–73	1977–78	1979–80	1980–81	1981–82	1982–83
HOME AND OVERSEAS TOTAL[1]	95	112	115	115	113	109
of which: Undergraduates	66	81	84	85	82	79
: Postgraduates	29	31	31	30	31	30
Taught	20	22	22	22	23	22
Research	9	9	9	8	8	8
HOME TOTAL[1,2]	N/A	93	97	100	99	95
of which: Undergraduates	62	73	77	79	77	74
: Postgraduates	N/A	19	20	21	21	21
Taught	N/A	14	14	15	16	15
Research	N/A	5	5	5	5	5
Mature undergraduate new entrants aged 21 and over[3]	10	14	13	13	13	12
As percentage of total undergraduate new entrants	15%	17%	16%	15%	15%	15%
OVERSEAS TOTAL [1,2]	N/A	19	18	15	14	15
of which: Undergraduates	4	8	7	5	5	5
: Postgraduates	N/A	11	11	10	9	9
Taught	N/A	8	8	7	7	7
Research	N/A	4	3	3	3	3
OVERSEAS TOTAL as percentage of all new entrants	N/A	17%	16%	13%	13%	13%

(NUMBERS MAY NOT SUM DUE TO ROUNDING)

[1] Includes transfers and secondments throughout.
[2] See Note 1 to Table 1.
[3] As at 31 December.
N/A = Not available.

GREAT BRITAIN

NEW ENTRANTS (FULL-TIME AND SANDWICH) — HOME AND OVERSEAS

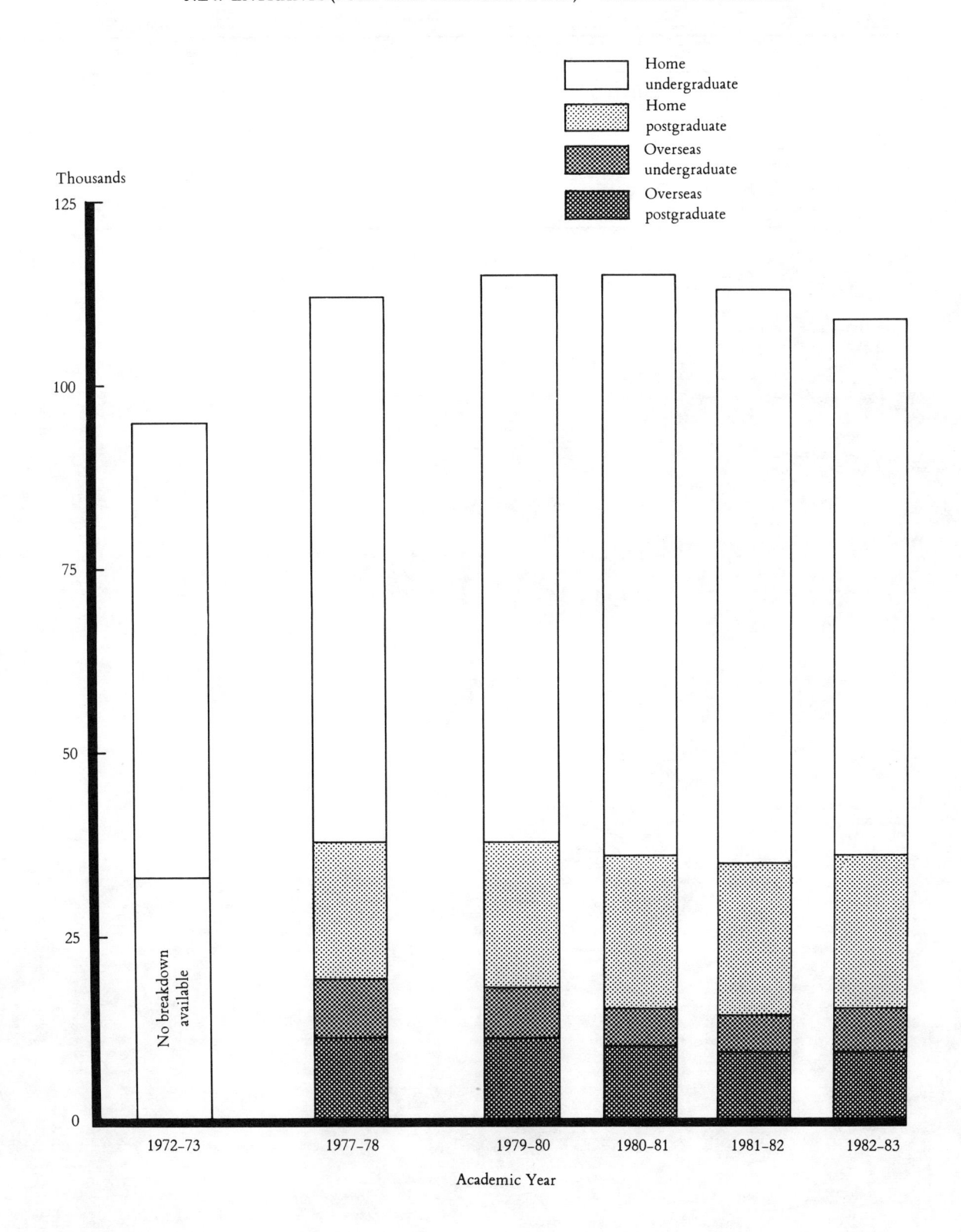

□ Home undergraduate
▒ Home postgraduate
▓ Overseas undergraduate
■ Overseas postgraduate

Thousands

Academic Year

GREAT BRITAIN

Annex G: Table 3

STUDENT NUMBERS (PART-TIME) — HOME AND OVERSEAS

THOUSANDS

	1965–66	1972–73	1977–78	1979–80	1980–81	1981–82	1982–83
HOME AND OVERSEAS PART-TIME TOTAL	17	23	27	30	32	33	34
of which: Undergraduates	5	3	4	4	4	5	5
: Postgraduates	12	20	23	26	27	28	28
of which: Men	14	17	19	21	22	22	22
: Women	3	5	8	9	10	11	12
Women as percentage of total	17%	23%	30%	32%	33%	34%	36%

(NUMBERS MAY NOT SUM DUE TO ROUNDING)

Annex G: Table 4

GREAT BRITAIN

HOME STUDENT NUMBERS (FULL-TIME AND SANDWICH) — SUBJECT OF STUDY

UNDERGRADUATES	1972-73	1977-78	1979-80	1980-81	1981-82	1982-83
Education	604	2,516	3,446	3,360	3,460	3,349
Pre-clinical medicine and dentistry	9,717	9,467	9,493	9,221	9,253	9,372
Clinical medicine	6,237	8,827	9,529	10,074	10,230	10,252
Clinical dentistry	1,734	2,707	2,756	2,808	2,817	2,875
Other studies allied to medicine and health	3,255	4,357	4,736	4,748	4,674	4,586
Engineering	25,398	24,708	27,274	28,893	29,902	29,830
Other technologies	1,336	1,652	1,764	1,839	1,921	2,029
Agriculture	2,131	2,894	3,395	3,360	3,382	3,306
Veterinary science	1,231	1,602	1,639	1,651	1,675	1,684
Biological sciences	18,453	18,014	18,360	19,037	18,802	18,154
Mathematics	10,197	9,526	10,553	11,843	13,004	13,670
Physical sciences	18,668	21,642	23,213	23,968	24,882	25,287
Business management	1,734	2,843	3,281	3,635	3,962	3,929
Social studies	38,525	49,215	51,714	53,040	52,842	51,495
Architecture and town planning	2,489	3,132	2,934	3,003	2,984	2,934
Other professional and vocational studies	531	734	855	900	908	855
Arts	42,303	50,704	52,743	54,461	55,069	53,422
TOTAL	184,543	214,540	227,685	235,841	239,767	237,029

POSTGRADUATES	1972-73	1977-78	1979-80	1980-81	1981-82	1982-83
Education	7,358	6,884	6,902	7,441	7,458	6,699
Pre-clinical medicine and dentistry	278	274	302	326	316	284
Clinical medicine	844	912	996	1,126	1,150	1,209
Clinical dentistry	74	78	67	59	60	62
Other studies allied to medicine and health	485	531	549	519	543	586
Engineering	3,099	2,270	2,133	2,251	2,613	2,759
Other technologies	766	621	585	610	699	688
Agriculture	464	403	424	436	461	445
Veterinary science	76	65	64	61	75	73
Biological sciences	2,476	2,428	2,494	2,514	2,439	2,391
Mathematics	1,301	1,048	1,032	1,110	1,206	1,172
Physical sciences	4,698	4,056	3,860	3,975	3,985	4,071
Business management	1,354	1,246	1,265	1,374	1,504	1,529
Social studies	4,705	5,197	4,972	5,230	5,324	4,937
Architecture and town planning	711	662	552	552	570	565
Other professional and vocational studies	210	391	350	379	288	297
Arts	4,115	3,728	3,646	3,708	3,572	3,372
TOTAL	33,014	30,794	30,193	31,671	32,263	31,139

(NUMBERS MAY NOT SUM DUE TO ROUNDING)

Annex G: Table 5

GREAT BRITAIN

HOME[1] STUDENT NUMBERS (FULL-TIME AND SANDWICH) — ARTS, SCIENCES, MEDICINE[2]

THOUSANDS

	ARTS	SCIENCE	MEDICINE	TOTAL
FULL-TIME AND SANDWICH TOTAL				
1972–73	101	97	19	218
1977–78	123	100	22	245
1979–80	129	106	23	258
1980–81	134	110	24	268
1981–82	134	114	24	272
1982–83	130	114	24	268
FULL-TIME AND SANDWICH UNDERGRADUATES				
1972–73	84	83	18	185
1977–78	106	88	21	215
1979–80	112	94	22	228
1980–81	115	98	22	236
1981–82	116	101	22	240
1982–83	113	101	23	237
FULL-TIME AND SANDWICH POSTGRADUATES				
1972–73	18	14	1	33
1977–78	17	12	1	31
1979–80	17	12	1	30
1980–81	18	12	2	32
1981–82	18	13	2	32
1982–83	17	13	2	31

(NUMBERS MAY NOT SUM DUE TO ROUNDING)

[1] See note 1 to Table 1.

[2] The subjects of study listed in Table 4 are grouped in the following way:—

Arts: education, business management, social studies, other professional and vocational studies, arts.

Science: other studies allied to medicine and health, engineering, other technologies, agriculture, veterinary science, biological sciences, mathematics, physical sciences, architecture and town planning.

Medicine: pre-clinical medicine and dentistry, clinical medicine, clinical dentistry.

GREAT BRITAIN

PERCENTAGE OF FULL TIME AND SANDWICH HOME UNDERGRADUATES
(with number of students in thousands)

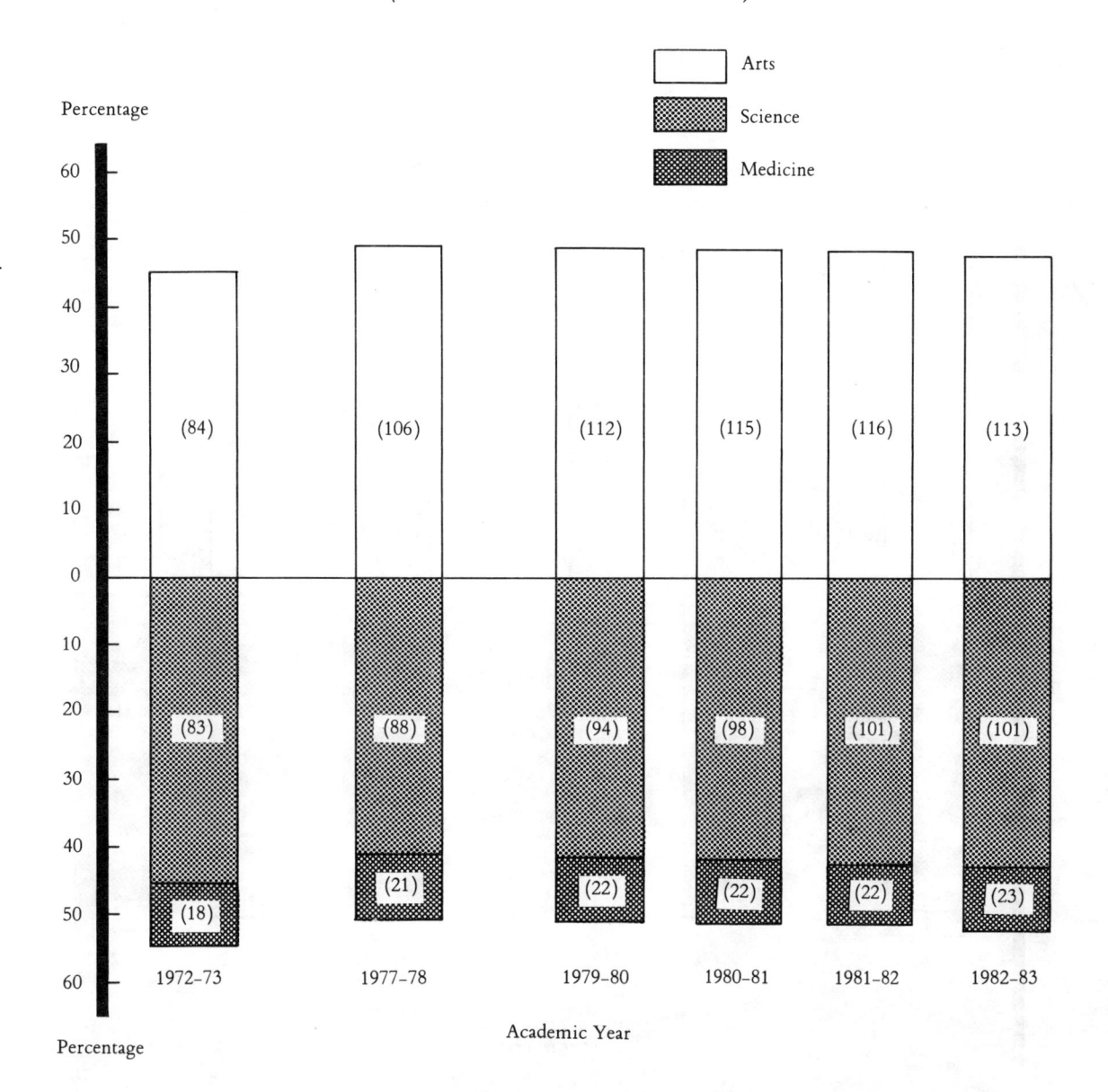

Academic Year	Arts	Science	Medicine
1972–73	(84)	(83)	(18)
1977–78	(106)	(88)	(21)
1979–80	(112)	(94)	(22)
1980–81	(115)	(98)	(22)
1981–82	(116)	(101)	(22)
1982–83	(113)	(101)	(23)

GREAT BRITAIN

PERCENTAGE OF FULL TIME AND SANDWICH HOME POSTGRADUATES
(with number of students in thousands)

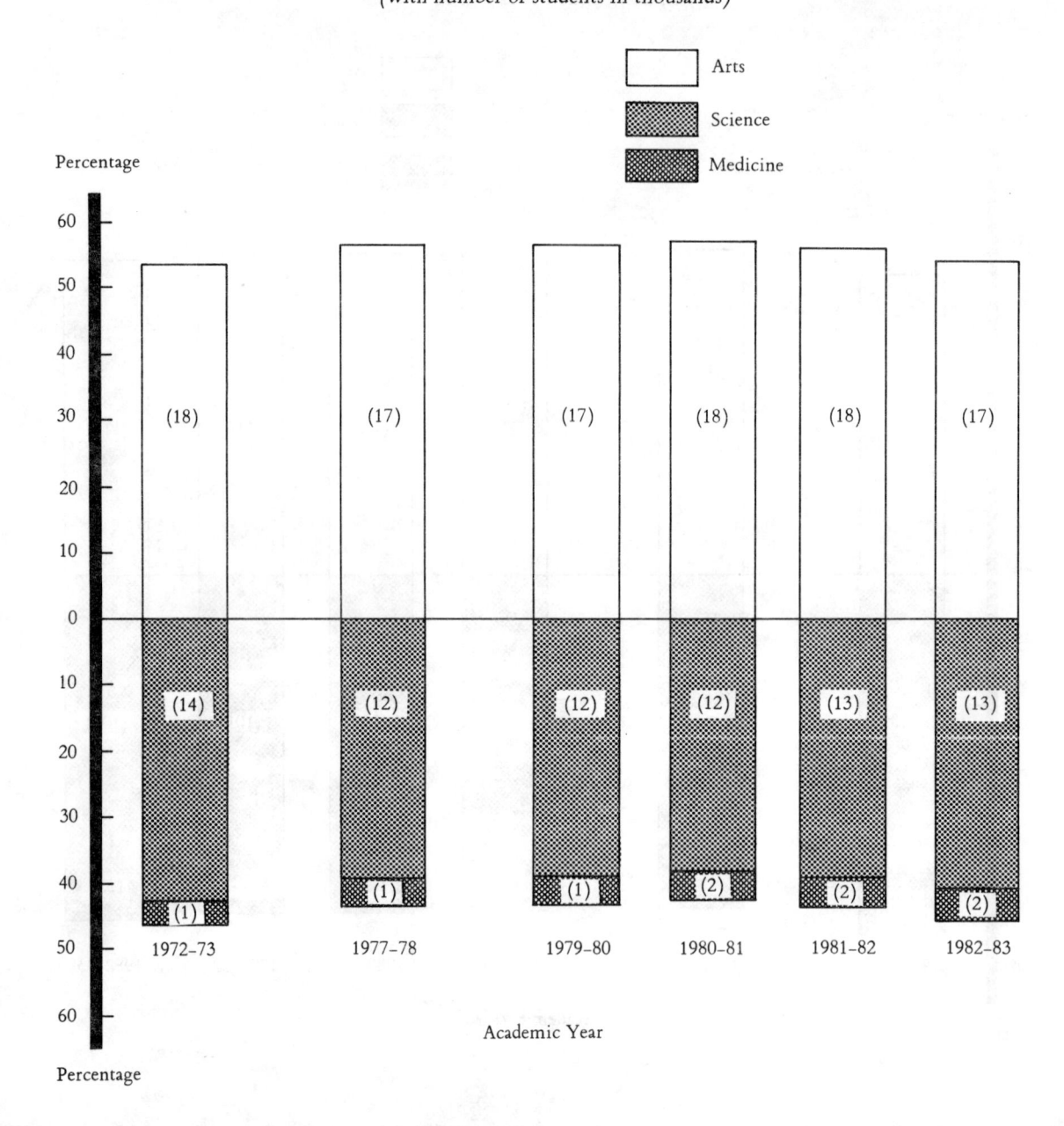

Academic Year	Arts	Science	Medicine
1972-73	(18)	(14)	(1)
1977-78	(17)	(12)	(1)
1979-80	(17)	(12)	(1)
1980-81	(18)	(12)	(2)
1981-82	(18)	(13)	(2)
1982-83	(17)	(13)	(2)

Annex G: Table 6

GREAT BRITAIN

CONTINUING EDUCATION

	NUMBER OF STUDENTS	NUMBER OF COURSES	NUMBER OF STUDENT HOURS[1]
	(Thousands)	(Thousands)	(Millions)
TOTAL: ALL COURSES			
1977–78	373	15.6	9.9
1979–80	382	16.0	10.2
1980–81	399	17.3	10.0
1981–82	443	18.8	11.4
1982–83	449	19.2	10.9
EXTRAMURAL COURSES (including joint courses with WEA[2])			
1977–78	220	9.9	5.5
1979–80	230	10.3	5.7
1980–81	239	10.9	5.8
1981–82	253	11.5	5.9
1982–83	266	12.1	5.9
POSTGRADUATE MEDICAL AND DENTAL COURSES			
1977–78	74	3.0	1.9
1979–80	68	2.8	1.8
1980–81	75	3.4	1.7
1981–82	85	3.5	2.4
1982–83	76	3.1	1.9
OTHER COURSES			
1977–78	80	2.6	2.6
1979–80	83	2.9	2.7
1980–81	86	3.0	2.5
1981–82	105	3.9	3.1
1982–83	107	4.1	3.1

(NUMBERS MAY NOT SUM DUE TO ROUNDING)

[1] Student hours are calculated for each course on the basis of the contact hours recorded for the aggregated student attendances.

[2] Workers Educational Association.

Annex G: Table 7

UCCA[1]—APPLICATIONS AND ACCEPTANCES (UNITED KINGDOM)

	As at October		
	1981[3]	1982[4]	1983[4]
1. Home[2] candidates for admission to UK universities through UCCA	149,330	156,675	157,015
2. Home[2] candidates accepted by UK universities through UCCA	74,514	72,634	69,631
3. Proportion of home candidates accepted	49.9%	46.4%	44.3%
4. Home[2] candidates who re-applied[5]	19,830	22,490	21,670
5. All candidates for admission to UK universities through UCCA	167,096	171,496	172,738
6. All candidates accepted by UK universities through UCCA	80,341	77,752	74,860
7. Proportion of all candidates accepted	48.1%	45.3%	43.3%

[1] The Universities' Central Council on Admissions.
[2] Domicile. (Prior to 1981 figures were on a fee-paying basis).
[3] Aberdeen, Glasgow and Strathclyde universities partly outwith the UCCA scheme.
[4] Glasgow and Strathclyde universities partly outwith the UCCA scheme.
[5] Figures scaled up from the results of a 10% sample.

Annex G: Table 8

A-LEVEL MEAN SCORES[1] OF NEW HOME ENTRANTS (FULL-TIME AND SANDWICH)—ENGLAND AND WALES[2]

SUBJECT GROUP	1972–73	1977–78	1979–80	1980–81	1981–82	1982–83
Education	8.6	6.3	7.3	7.4	7.1	8.1
Medicine, dentistry and health	10.2	11.3	11.4	11.5	11.8	12.0
Engineering and technology	8.8	9.0	9.5	9.7	10.2	10.6
Agriculture, forestry and veterinary science	8.3	9.2	9.4	9.4	9.5	9.7
Science	9.7	9.3	9.5	9.7	10.1	10.6
Social administrative and business studies	10.1	9.6	9.5	9.5	10.0	10.3
Architecture and other professional and vocational subjects	9.3	9.7	9.2	9.2	9.6	9.9
Language, literature and area studies	10.8	10.1	10.1	10.2	10.5	10.9
Arts other than languages	10.1	9.2	9.2	9.4	9.6	10.0
OVERALL	9.9	9.6	9.7	9.8	10.2	10.6

[1] A-grade scores 5, B-grade scores 4 and so on. The best three grades have been taken for students with passes in more than three subjects.

[2] It is not possible to provide a satisfactory analogous table for Scotland because there is no agreed method of equating performances in A-levels with performances in Scottish Highers.

Annex G: Table 9

GREAT BRITAIN

STUDENT : STAFF RATIOS[1]

DEPARTMENT	1967–68[2]	1972–73	1977–78	1979–80	1980–81	1981–82	1982–83
TOTAL	8.3	8.4	9.2	9.3	9.4	9.7	10.1
ARTS[3]	10.1	9.9	10.9	10.9	11.0	11.2	11.5
SCIENCE[3]	7.6	7.7	8.6	8.8	9.0	9.2	9.8
CLINICAL[3]	5.5	5.3	5.5	5.4	5.6	5.8	6.4
Education	12.5	11.6	11.9	11.3	11.2	11.4	11.3
Pre-clinical studies	6.0	—[4]	8.7	8.4	8.3	8.8	8.8
Clinical medicine	5.7	5.3	5.4	5.3	5.6	5.9	6.6
Clinical dentistry	6.4	5.7	6.2	6.2	6.1	5.9	6.3
Studies allied to medicine	7.1	6.5	9.5	9.5	9.6	10.1	10.4
Engineering	8.0	7.9	9.0	9.3	9.3	9.5	10.2
Other technologies	4.9	9.9	9.0	8.4	8.9	9.3	9.9
Agriculture	5.2	7.1	9.9	10.2	9.6	9.5	10.2
Veterinary science	3.7	4.1	5.0	5.0	4.8	5.0	5.4
Biological sciences	7.0	—[4]	8.4	8.9	8.9	8.7	9.1
Mathematics	9.0	9.4	9.6	10.6	11.2	11.4	12.3
Physical sciences	7.9	7.1	7.2	7.4	7.6	7.8	8.4
Business management	10.9	8.0	10.7	10.7	10.7	11.5	12.8
Social studies	11.3	10.9	11.9	11.6	11.8	11.9	12.1
Architecture and town planning	10.0	9.5	9.5	8.9	8.4	8.8	9.6
Other professional and vocational	6.7	9.6	9.4	9.9	11.9	11.7	11.5
Arts	8.9	9.1	10.0	10.3	10.4	10.5	10.9

[1] The ratio of the full-time equivalent student load on the department to the number of full-time staff in that department — counting home and overseas students and staff paid wholly from university funds.
[2] Prior years used different subject groupings.
[3] Departments are grouped in the following way:—
Arts: education, business management, social studies, other professional and vocational studies, arts.
Science: pre-clinical studies, studies allied to medicine, engineering, other technologies, agriculture, biological sciences, mathematics, physical sciences, architecture and town planning.
Clinical: clinical medicine, clinical dentistry, veterinary science.
[4] Ratios omitted because the allocation of student load to these two departmental groups in 1972–73 was inconsistent with the allocation of staff.

GREAT BRITAIN

STUDENT: STAFF RATIOS

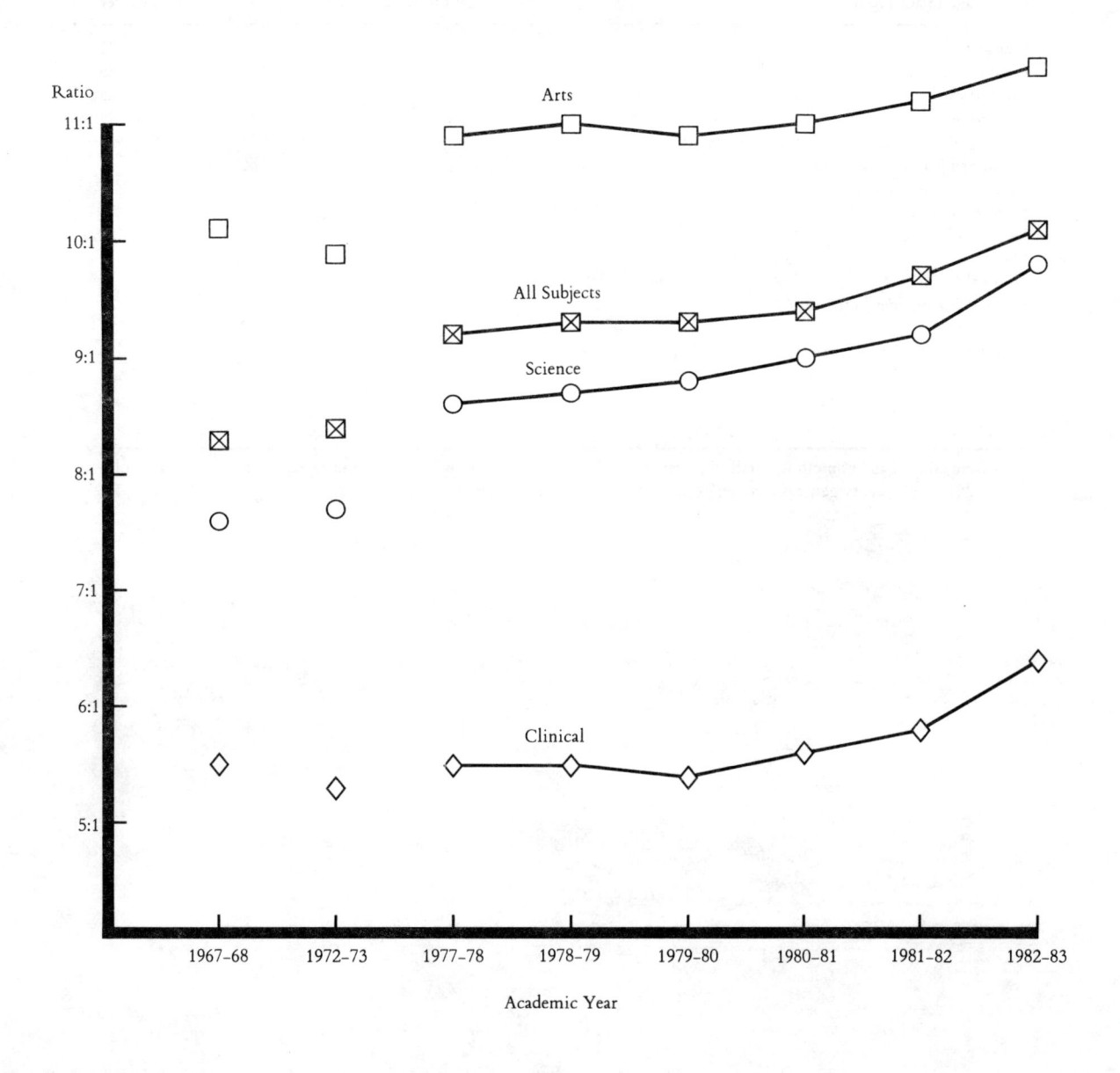

Ratio

Arts

All Subjects

Science

Clinical

Academic Year: 1967–68, 1972–73, 1977–78, 1978–79, 1979–80, 1980–81, 1981–82, 1982–83

◇ Clinical
○ Science
□ Arts
⊠ All Subjects

Annex G: Table 10

AGE DISTRIBUTION OF ACADEMIC STAFF[1] IN GB UNIVERSITIES: 1982–83

Percentage in age groups	under 35	35–49	50 and over
Education	6	59	35
Pre-clinical medicine and dentistry	21	54	25
Clinical medicine	25	50	25
Clinical dentistry	21	50	29
Studies allied to medicine, dentistry and health	22	53	25
Engineering and other technologies	12	56	32
Agriculture and forestry	16	50	34
Veterinary science	21	42	37
Biological sciences	16	58	26
Mathematical sciences including computer science	17	64	19
Physical sciences	10	59	31
Business management studies	20	59	22
Social studies	25	57	18
Architecture and town planning	12	58	30
Other professional and vocational studies	16	50	34
Arts	15	59	26
All subjects	17	57	26

[1] Full-time clinical and non-clinical staff in academic grades whose function is "teaching and research" and who are wholly financed from university general income: excludes staff in adult education departments.